FACTS AT YOUR
FINGERTIPS

INTRODUCING PHYSICS
MATTER, ENERGY, AND HEAT

BROWN
BEAR
BOOKS

Published by Brown Bear Books Limited

4877 N. Circulo Bujia
Tucson, AZ 85718
USA
and
First Floor
9-17 St. Albans Place
London N1 ONX
UK
www.brownreference.com

© 2010 The Brown Reference Group Ltd

Library of Congress Cataloging-in-Publication Data

Matter, energy, and heat / edited by Graham Bateman.
    p. cm. – (Facts at your fingertips)
  Includes index.
  ISBN 978-1-936333-05-9 (lib. bdg.)
  1. Heat-Transmission–Juvenile literature. 2. Physics–Juvenile literature. I.
Bateman, Graham. II. Title: Matter, energy, and heat. III. Series.

QC320.14.I58 2010
530–dc22

2010015426

ISBN-13 978-1-936333-05-9

Editorial Director: Lindsey Lowe
Project Director: Graham Bateman
Design Manager: David Poole
Designer: Steve McCurdy
Text Editor: Peter Lewis
Indexer: David Bennett
Children's Publisher: Anne O'Daly
Production Director: Alastair Gourlay

Printed in the United States of America

Picture Credits
Abbreviations: SS=Shutterstock; c=center; t=top; l=left; r=right.

Cover Images
Front: SS: James Doss Back: SS: hardtmuth
1 SS: Stephanie Swartz; 3 Photos.com; 4-5 SS: Mopic; 6-7 SS: Bobby
Dailey; 9 Photos.com; 10 Photos.com; 12 SS: Cardaf; 13 Photos.com;
16 SS: E. G. Pors; 17 SS: Thoron; 19 SS: hfng; 20-21 SS: Stephanie
Swartz; 23 SS: Juerg Schtreiter; 24-25 SS: Dragan Trifunovic; 26 SS:
Can Balcioglu; 28-29 SS: Zastoloskiy Voctor Leonidovich; 33 SS: Yusia;
36-37 SS: Michael Coddington; 38-39 SS: Linda M. Foster; 41
Photos.com; 43 SS: Styve Reineck; 45 SS: Lilybranch; 46 Photos.com;
49 SS: Palms; 54 SS: Christine Gonsalves; 56-57 SS: Four Oakes; 58-59
SS: A cotton Photo; 60-61 SS: Peter Gudella.

CONTENTS

Artwork © The Brown Reference Group Ltd

*The Brown Reference Group Ltd has made every effort to trace
copyright holders of the pictures used in this book. Anyone having
claims to ownership not identified above is invited to contact The
Brown Reference Group Ltd.*

Facts at your Fingertips—Introducing Physics describes the processes and practical implications fundamental to the study of physics. *Matter, Energy, and Heat* introduces the various states of matter (solid, liquid, or gas) found in the world around us, describes its constituents, and discusses the various physical factors that influence it, such as the effects of pressure. Heat is a form of energy, with temperature a measure of the hotness of an object. The effects of heat on solids, liquids, and gases are described, including the processes involved when a substance changes from one state to another. This is followed by an account of the three ways in which heat can travel from one place to another through conduction, convection, and radiation, including the properties of good and bad conductors.

Numerous explanatory diagrams and informative photographs, detailed features on related aspects of the topics covered and the main scientists involved in the advancement of physics, and definitions of key "Science Words," all enhance the coverage. "Try This" features outline experiments that can be undertaken as a first step to practical investigations.

ATOMS AND MOLECULES

Everything in the world is made up of tiny particles. The smallest particles that can exist on their own are called atoms. Often, atoms join together to form larger particles called molecules. All chemical compounds are made up of molecules.

There are just over 100 different chemical elements, each with its own kinds of atom. Most elements are metals, such as iron, copper, and aluminum. A piece of iron is made up of millions and millions of iron atoms. Some elements are gases, such as oxygen and hydrogen. Only two elements are liquid at ordinary temperatures. They are the silvery liquid metal mercury and a poisonous reddish brown liquid that is called bromine.

The characteristics of substances formed when atoms of different elements combine are often very different from those of the individual elements. For instance, when the metal copper combines with the gas

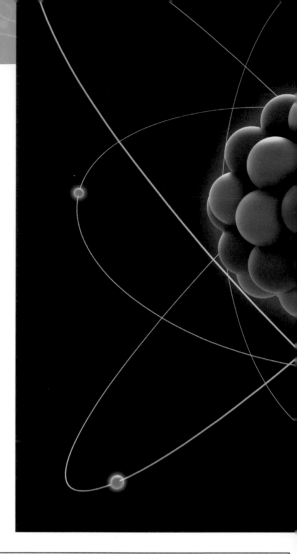

CHEMICAL BONDING

In ionic bonding, one atom gives one or more electrons to another atom to form a chemical compound that consists of ions. Here sodium and chlorine combine to make sodium chloride. In covalent bonding, the atoms share electrons. Here an oxygen atom shares electrons with two hydrogen atoms to form a molecule of water.

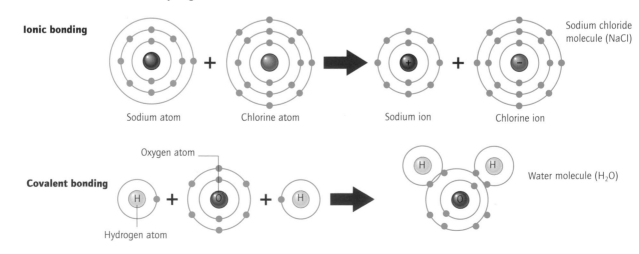

Ionic bonding

Sodium atom   Chlorine atom   Sodium ion   Chlorine ion

Sodium chloride molecule (NaCl)

Oxygen atom

Covalent bonding

Hydrogen atom

Water molecule (H_2O)

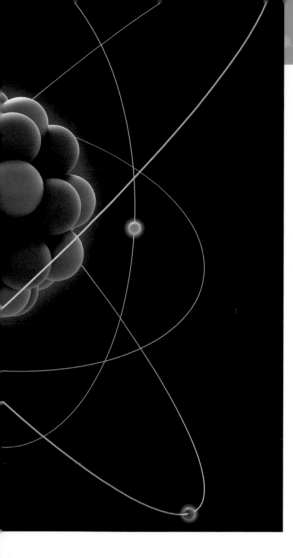

Simple model of an atom, showing the central core, or nucleus, surrounded by orbiting electrons.

oxygen, it forms molecules of the nonmetal copper oxide. And the two gases hydrogen and oxygen combine to form the liquid we know as water.

Atoms have structure

Atoms are not solid balls of matter. They consist of a central core, or nucleus, surrounded by one or more electrons. Electrons are therefore even smaller than the smallest atom—about one two-thousandth the size. Also, each electron carries a single negative electrical charge. The nucleus of the atom is also charged. Nuclei have a positive charge that balances the negative charges of the electrons. The electrons in an atom are arranged around the nucleus in layers called shells, like the layers inside an onion.

DIFFERENT KINDS OF CARBON

The element carbon exists in two different forms. In graphite, which is black and very soft, the atoms are linked in layers that slide easily over one another. But in diamond, the rigid structure forms the hardest crystals known.

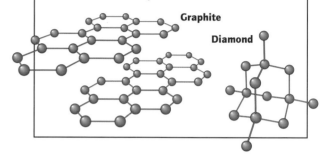

The joining of atoms to form molecules involves the electrons. There are two main ways this can happen. Some kinds of atom—chiefly metals—can lose one or more electrons. This leaves them with a positive charge, and charged atoms are called ions. Other kinds of atom—mainly nonmetals—can gain one or more electrons. This gives them a negative charge, and they become negative ions. If a metal such as sodium reacts with a nonmetal such as chlorine, each sodium atom gives an electron to a chlorine atom. They combine to form a molecule of sodium chloride, or table salt.

In another way of joining atoms, the electrons do not move from one atom to the other. Instead, atoms share electrons. When hydrogen reacts with oxygen, they share electrons to form a molecule of water.

SCIENCE WORDS

- **Atom:** The smallest part of a chemical element that can exist on its own. It has a central nucleus (made up of protons and neutrons), surrounded by electrons.
- **Molecule:** A combination of at least two atoms that forms the smallest unit of a chemical element or compound.

BEHAVIOR OF GASES

Like all kinds of matter, a gas is made up of atoms or molecules. But these particles do not stand still. They rush around, hitting one another and the walls of their container. As they collide with the container, gas pressure arises.

Gases make up one of the three states of matter—the other two are liquids and solids. We are surrounded by gas all the time because the air we breathe is a gas. In fact, air is a mixture of gases, mostly nitrogen and oxygen. You cannot see air, yet it has mass, and it exerts a pressure on everything in contact with it.

The weight of air

The air in an average room weighs about 175 lb (about 80 kg). The weight of all the air in the atmosphere totals many millions of tons, and it presses on everything in it. At sea level this atmospheric pressure is about 14 lb per square inch of surface (about 1 kg per sq. cm).

The pressure of the atmosphere can be measured using a barometer. There are various kinds. The Italian scientist Evangelista Torricelli (1608-1647) invented the first barometer in 1644. He took a long glass tube closed at one end and filled it with mercury. He then turned the tube upside down and lowered the open end into a bowl of mercury. The mercury did not all flow out of the tube. Its level fell slightly but then stopped, and the rest of the mercury remained in the tube. Torricelli reasoned that it was the atmosphere pressing on the surface of the mercury in the bowl that held up the column of mercury. The space above the mercury in the closed end of the tube contained no air at all.

Predicting the weather

Normal atmospheric pressure will hold up a column of mercury about 30 in (76 cm) tall. Because atmospheric pressure varies from day to day (because of the weather), the height of the mercury column also varies. People soon learned how to forecast the weather by watching the changes in pressure as revealed by a barometer. Clear, dry weather, for example, can usually be expected when the atmospheric pressure is on the increase. When the atmospheric pressure is falling, on the other hand, this generally indicates rainy weather.

Atmospheric pressure also decreases with height above the ground. It falls about 0.4 in (about 1 cm) for every 328-ft (100-meter) increase in height. Barometers can therefore be used for measuring altitude. Many of the altimeters carried by aircraft are sensitive barometers. They are usually the aneroid type ("aneroid" comes from Greek words meaning "no

SCIENCE WORDS

- **Atmospheric pressure:** The pressure of the Earth's atmosphere at any point on its surface (caused by the weight of the column of air above it). Atmospheric pressure decreases with altitude (height above ground).
- **Boyle's law:** At constant temperature the pressure of a gas is inversely proportional to its volume. For example, if the pressure increases, then the volume decreases.
- **Gas:** A state of matter in which the molecules move at random. A gas in a container takes on the size and shape of the container.
- **Pressure:** The amount of force pressing on a particular area.

liquid"). An aneroid barometer does not contain mercury. The heart of the instrument is a closed chamber containing no air. As the external air pressure varies, the small vacuum chamber changes shape, operating a system of levers to move a pointer that indicates the value of the pressure on a dial. In an altimeter, the dial is calibrated in height, not in pressure.

Other kinds of gas

Not all gases are as dense as air. Two light gases are hydrogen and helium. Hydrogen is dangerously flammable. It was once used for filling balloons and airships, but it stopped being used after there were several disastrous fires. The most famous accident was the explosion of the German airship *Hindenburg* in 1937. Modern airships are filled with helium. This gas is less dense than air, which is why a helium-filled balloon or airship floats upward in the air.

Helium is one of the two gases that are less dense than air—the other is hydrogen. But unlike hydrogen, helium does not burn. It is used to fill weather balloons and airships.

Other gases are used as fuels. Methane occurs underground in natural gas. The similar gases ethane and butane are obtained from crude oil in an oil refinery. They are sold as bottled gas for heating and lighting in campers and trailers. The same gases are also known as LPG (liquefied petroleum gas) and are being used as a cleaner alternative to gasoline for automobile engines.

Acetylene is a fuel gas that is burned in oxygen in an oxyacetylene torch. The very hot flame is employed for welding and cutting steel and other metals. The acetylene gas is liquefied and supplied in steel cylinders. Carbon dioxide is a very dense gas. Nothing will burn in carbon dioxide, which is why it is used in fire extinguishers.

Properties of gases

A gas that is confined within a closed container exerts a pressure. That is because the rapidly moving molecules of gas collide with the walls of the container. It is also why we have to keep the container closed—a gas will soon escape from an open container. If we decrease the volume of gas by making the container smaller, the pressure of the gas increases. For instance, the pressure doubles if we halve the size of the container. This relationship between gas pressure and volume was discovered by the British scientist Robert Boyle (1627–1691) and for this reason is known as Boyle's law.

Heating a gas also increases the pressure as long as the volume is kept the same. That is because the hotter

BOYLE'S LAW

The diagrams show the effect of increasing the pressure on a gas. When the pressure (P) is increased from 1 bar to 2 bars, the volume (V) is halved from 8 cu m to 4 cu m. Increasing the pressure to 4 bars reduces the volume to only 2 cu m. In other words, pressure is inversely proportional to volume. Put another way, the product of pressure and volume is constant.

Pressure = 1 bar

Volume = 8 cu m
P x V = 1 x 8 = 8

Pressure = 2 bars

Volume = 4 cu m
P x V = 2 x 4 = 8

Pressure = 4 bars

Volume = 2 cu m
P x V = 4 x 2 = 8

An oxyacetylene welder at work. Acetylene gas burns in oxygen with an extremely hot flame, which can be used for cutting or welding metal. The welder wears dark glasses to protect his eyes from the bright light of the torch.

gas molecules move faster and collide with the walls more often. If the volume is not kept constant, heating a gas causes it to expand and take up more room. An expanding gas can be made to do work, and several kinds of machine, for instance the steam engine and the jackhammer, make use of this fact.

A flow of gas can also be made to do work. The earliest device that made use of moving gas was the

Robert Boyle

Robert Boyle was born in Munster, Ireland, in 1627, son of the Earl of Cork. He studied abroad in Switzerland before returning to England in 1644, settling in Oxford ten years later. He carried out many experiments in both physics and chemistry. Boyle investigated electricity, crystals, and relative density. He invented an air pump and studied the effects of pressure on gases. In 1662, he formulated Boyle's law: At constant temperature, the pressure of a gas is inversely proportional to its volume. He later moved to London and became a founder member of the Royal Society in 1662. He was a great believer in finding practical uses for science. Boyle died in 1691.

sailing ship, where the moving gas is the wind. Later, people harnessed the wind with windmills. Many windmills had sails that resemble those on a sailing ship, and windmills like this can still be seen in Mediterranean countries such as Spain and Greece.

MERCURY MANOMETER

A simple device for measuring gas pressures is called a manometer. It consists of a U-shaped glass tube containing mercury. One end of the tube is open to the air, and the other end is connected to the gas supply. The pressure of the gas forces mercury up the open arm of the manometer. The difference in heights of the mercury columns is a measure of the pressure.

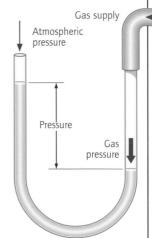

Gas supply

Atmospheric pressure

Pressure

Gas pressure

BEHAVIOR OF LIQUIDS

Liquids are the "middle" state of matter. They are denser than gases, but not as dense as solids. And like gases, they flow readily and so have to be kept in a container.

The molecules that make up a liquid are free to move around. That is why a liquid has no definite shape—it just takes up the shape of its container. The container does not need a lid to prevent the liquid from escaping (unlike a gas). Also unlike a gas, a liquid cannot be compressed: increasing the pressure on a liquid does not make it occupy a smaller volume. But a liquid does exert a pressure on the sides and bottom of its container (and on anything that happens to be in it), and this pressure depends on the liquid's density

CAPILLARY ACTION

The shape of the meniscus in a capillary tube depends on the density of the liquid and its ability to wet the glass. Water has a concave (curved downward) meniscus; mercury has a convex (curved upward) meniscus.

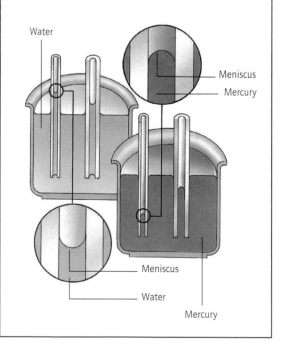

Water

Meniscus

Mercury

Meniscus

Water

Mercury

and its depth. The greater the depth of a liquid, the greater the pressure.

Another property of a liquid is called viscosity, which is a measure of how thick it is. Machine oil and molasses are viscous liquids, which flow only slowly. Water and alcohol are not viscous, and they flow easily. This is because the molecules in water, for instance, slide past one another much more easily than do the molecules in molasses.

Surface tension and capillarity

The molecules at the surface of a liquid attract one another. This causes an effect, called surface tension, that makes the liquid behave as if it had an elastic "skin" on its surface. It makes it possible to float a needle on the surface of water in a glass and allows bugs such as pond skaters to walk across the surface of a pond. It is also the reason why bubbles and liquid droplets are spherical.

Water is the commonest liquid on Earth. Here a "water bomber" aircraft drops water on a forest fire in an attempt to put it out.

A substance called a surfactant, also known as a wetting agent, can reduce surface tension. Detergents are surfactants, and adding them to washing water allows the water to get into small crevices in closely woven cloth and pry away any dirt that may be lodged there.

Another effect of surface tension is called capillary action, or capillarity. It is this effect that makes blotting paper or a sponge soak up water. It can be observed by lowering a narrow glass tube vertically into a liquid. With a liquid such as water, the liquid rises up the tube a little way. If you look closely at the surface of the liquid inside the tube, you will see that it is curved—it is higher at the sides of the tube than at the center. This curve, called a meniscus, is saucer-shaped in the case of water. But in a dense liquid such as mercury, it is curved upward—higher at the center than at the sides.

SCIENCE WORDS

- **Capillarity:** Also called capillary action, the movement of a liquid up or down a narrow tube, caused by the attraction between its molecules and those of the tube. The surface of the liquid is curved into a meniscus.
- **Meniscus:** The curved shape of the surface of a liquid in a narrow tube, caused by capillarity.
- **Surface tension:** An effect that makes a liquid appear to have a surface "skin."

TRY THIS

Scatter powder
The surface of water behaves as if it has a skin over it. The skin is strong enough to support bugs and other water insects that can walk on water. But what happens to such floating objects if you stretch the skin?

What to do
Take a large shallow bowl, make sure it is perfectly clean, and fill it nearly to the top with water. When the surface is still and smooth, sprinkle a little talcum powder on it. Put a small smear of liquid detergent on the end of your finger, and gently touch the water near the center of the bowl. The talcum powder will immediately rush away from your finger toward the edges of the bowl.

The detergent breaks the water's surface tension so that it can no longer support the particles of powder. The "skin" on the unaffected water near the edges of the dish pulls away, carrying the powder with it, though it looks as if your finger is pushing it away. You must thoroughly wash away all the detergent from the bowl and dry it carefully if you want to repeat the experiment.

Touch the surface of the water with detergent, and watch the powder scatter.

SOLIDS AND CRYSTALS

The atoms and molecules that make up solids are hardly able to move at all. They are held in a regular arrangement, which is responsible for the regular shapes of crystals.

Most solids are hard, rigid, and strong, and many have high melting points. All these properties reflect the fact that their atoms are held together by strong interatomic forces. But some solids consist of large molecules held together by only weak intermolecular forces. They tend to be soft and have low melting points. Waxes and many polymers (plastics) are typical examples.

Crystals are solids in which the component atoms or molecules are arranged in a regular, repeating pattern

The expression "solid as a rock" is used to describe anything that is very solid. Dams are made of concrete, which is like artificial rock. It is solid enough to hold back the millions of tons of water in the lake behind it.

called a lattice. When a crystalline solid is heated, its particles hold their positions in the lattice until the melting point is reached, when the solid suddenly melts. A solid that lacks this kind of regular internal arrangement of its particles is termed noncrystalline, or amorphous. Glass and plastics are amorphous solids. When they are heated, they soften gradually over a wide range of temperatures and have no definite melting point.

The exact nature of the particles in a crystal varies among different materials. In most metals and some other solid elements such as sulfur, or carbon in the form of diamond, the crystals are made up of atoms. In substances such as sugar, the crystal components are molecules. But in the vast majority of crystalline substances the particles are ions. Nearly all salts and minerals—and therefore rocks—are basically ionic solids.

Metals are crystals

When we see the word "crystal," we tend to think of something clear and angular, like a sparkling diamond. Most metals are also made up of crystals. This fact, and the type of bonding between the particles within the crystals, explain most of the properties of metals.

A typical metal can be cut or polished to produce a shiny surface. Indeed, until people learned how to put a thin layer of silver on a sheet of glass, all mirrors were made of polished metal. Many metals can be drawn out so that the piece gets thinner and thinner to form wire. This property is called ductility, and we say that

Diamond is among the most valuable of crystals. It is also the hardest solid known. These diamonds have been cut and polished for use in jewelry.

CRYSTAL SYSTEMS

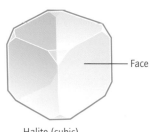

Halite (cubic)

Zircon (tetragonal)

Calcite (trigonal)

Beryl (hexagonal)

There are seven crystal systems (see page 15), illustrated here by means of seven common minerals. The external shape is called the crystal habit. All crystals of the same substance always have the same angles between their faces. But the habit may vary because different faces may grow at different speeds.

Kyanite (triclinic)

Gypsum (monoclinic)

Barytes (orthorhombic)

the metal is ductile. Many metals can also be hammered into thin sheets. Gold, for example, can be beaten into gold leaf so thin that light passes through it. This property is called malleability, and we say that the metal is malleable.

Some metals, such as copper and gold, are both ductile and malleable. They have these properties because, when they are stretched or hammered, their atoms slip past one another so that the solid can take up its new shape. The kind of bonding in metals must therefore be different from that in other crystalline solids. In a metal, the outermost electrons of the atoms easily become detached. This creates positive ions, which are surrounded by a "sea" of electrons. These electrons are free to move, and this accounts for the ability of a metal to conduct electricity. When a battery, for example, is connected across the ends of a piece of

CRYSTAL AXES

The different crystal systems are defined in terms of imaginary axes drawn inside them. Six of the systems have three axes. The simplest is the cubic system, which has three equal axes at right angles. The hexagonal system has four axes.

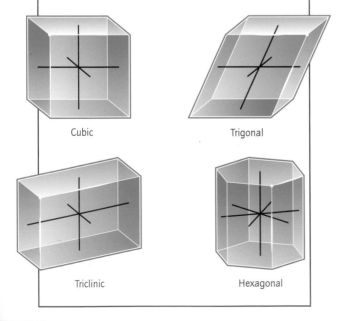

Cubic

Trigonal

Triclinic

Hexagonal

UNIT CELLS OF CRYSTALS

The basic arrangement of atoms or ions in a crystal is called a unit cell. It determines the outward shape of the crystal. These three examples are common among metals and other crystalline substances.

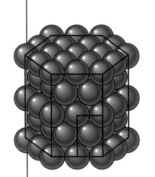

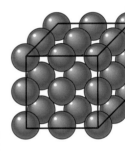

Face-centered cubic

Hexagonal close-packed

Body-centered cubic

metal wire, the electrons flow along the wire and produce an electric current. The free electrons also make metals good conductors of heat.

Bonding in solids

We have now identified four different kinds of bonds that hold together the particles in solids. In substances such as diamond, the atoms share electrons and are held together by covalent bonds (see the diagrams on page 4). In substances such as salt, the particles take the form of positive and negative ions held together by electrical attraction called ionic bonds. In a wax, the particles are molecules that are held together by intermolecular forces. And in a metal, the atoms are held together by metallic bonds involving free electrons. But despite their differences, all four types of solid can form crystals.

Classifying crystals

To early scientists, crystals presented a bewildering array of different forms. Natural mineral crystals come in all shapes, sizes, and colors. Gradually, scientists realized that there are seven basic crystal forms, and all crystals belong to one of them. But natural crystals are seldom perfect and may become distorted while they slowly form in the ground, or they may be affected by the presence of impurities. Throughout the ages people have valued gemstones such as diamonds, emeralds, and rubies for their beauty and rarity. Even today, collectors eagerly seek perfect specimens of ordinary mineral crystals.

The seven crystal forms are called systems (see page 13). Their names come from their geometrical shape. The simplest is the cube, which is represented in the cubic system. Common salt is found naturally as the mineral rock salt known to mineralogists as halite. It crystallizes as cubes. If you have a strong magnifying glass, you can use it to see the cubic shape of crystals of table salt.

Internal structure

The particles within a crystal are arranged in a regular pattern called the crystal lattice. Common salt is composed of ions, and in the common salt crystal the ions are arranged at the corners of cubes. Salt crystals are also cubes, so in this case the shape of the crystal reflects the arrangement of ions in the crystal lattice.

This is also true for many other crystal shapes. If you imagine eight ions at the corners of a cube, you can see that there is a space in the middle for another ion. This arrangement is the crystal lattice known as body-centered cubic. In another arrangement, there is an extra ion at the center of each face of the cube. This pattern is called face-centered cubic (see opposite).

In yet another arrangement, there is a circle of six ions with a seventh ion in the middle. Picture arranging seven oranges in this fashion. Now imagine adding three more oranges on top of this layer. You could then add another layer of six, and so on, to build up what is called a hexagonal close-packed arrangement.

Scientists investigate the structure of crystals using x-rays. When x-rays pass through a crystal, the atoms or ions scatter the rays and the pattern of the scattered x-rays can be recorded on a piece of photographic film. Because of the regular arrangement of particles within the crystal, the scattered x-rays create a distinctive pattern of spots on the photograph. From this pattern, the scientists can work out the crystal structure.

TRY THIS

Grow your own crystals
Mineral crystals form underground as molten material or concentrated solutions gradually cool. The slower they cool, the larger the crystals grow. Try growing your own crystals.

What to do
First take a crystalline substance—sugar, salt, and alum work well. Then add it to a jar of warm water until no more will dissolve. Tie or fix one crystal to the end of a piece of thin thread, and suspend it in the solution (tie the thread to a pencil across the top of the jar). Set it aside for several days. Gradually, the crystal will get larger as the substance comes out of solution. The new solid follows exactly the same shape as the original crystal as the particles take their regular places in the crystal lattice.

DENSITY AND FLOATING

Which is heavier: a piece of wood or a piece of steel? The answer depends on their sizes. A piece of wood the size of a table is heavier than a piece of steel the size of a pin. But a ton of wood weighs the same as a ton of steel.

A piece of steel may or may not be heavier than a piece of wood, depending on their sizes. But steel is always denser than wood. The density of a substance is its mass divided by its volume. Steel has a density of about 480 lb per cu ft (7,800 kg per cu m), while the density of wood is only about 44 lb per cu ft (700 kg per cu m), depending on the type of wood. So, on average steel is about 11 times as dense as wood.

Water has a density of 62 lb per cu ft (1,000 kg per cu m), higher than wood but much less than steel. That is why a piece of wood floats on water and a lump of steel sinks. Difference in densities is also why a balloon that is full of helium gas (density 0.01 lb per cu ft/0.18 kg per cu m) floats in air (density 0.08 lb per cu ft/1.3 kg per cu m).

For a piece of something to float, it must be less dense than the fluid—liquid or gas—it is floating in. Ice is less dense than water, which is why ice cubes float in a drink and icebergs float in the ocean. But ice is

Steel-hulled ships like this container carrier float because they are hollow. A ship displaces its own weight of water. It rides higher in the water when it has no cargo and sinks deeper when it is fully loaded because then it weighs more.

ICEBERGS FLOAT

Icebergs float because ice is less dense than seawater. The density of ice is about nine-tenths the density of water. For this reason, only 10 percent of the floating ice is above the water. The remaining 90 percent remains submerged.

only a little less dense than seawater, which is why the greater part of an iceberg stays below the surface, often jutting out underwater and being a danger to ships that get too close.

Sometimes scientists use relative density instead of density. It is equal to the density of a substance divided by the density of water. It is a pure number with no units. Thus gold has a density of 1,190 lb per cu ft (19,000 kg per cu m) and a relative density of 19 (equal to the density of gold divided by the density of water).

Density and strength

Steel is a very strong metal alloy. Aluminum is not quite so strong, but it is much less dense (170 lb per cu ft, or about 2,700 kg per cu m). For this reason, aluminum is used in space rockets and airplanes. A steel airplane would be three times as heavy as an aluminum one, and its engines would have to be three times as powerful to get it off the ground.

SCIENCE WORDS

- **Density:** For any substance its mass divided by its volume.
- **Upthrust:** The apparent loss in weight of a floating object, equal to the buoyant force keeping it afloat.

But some materials that have a low density are also strong. That is particularly true of composite materials like fiberglass and carbon fiber. Composite materials are made by combining two or more different materials to make a new material that is better in some way (usually stronger) than the ones it is made from. Fiberglass has thin hairlike strands of glass set in a plastic resin. It is slightly stronger than steel, but only one-fourth its density. It is used for making the hulls for small boats, for fishing rods, and for the poles used by pole-vaulters. Carbon fiber is a similar material but is even stronger.

Floating and displacement

One of the oldest stories in physics is about a Greek mathematician and scientist called Archimedes, who lived more than 2,200 years ago. According to the story, he decided to take a bath and climbed into a tub that was full to the brim with water. Of course, as soon as he got in, the water overflowed onto the floor. But Archimedes (c. 287–212 B.C.) was so pleased with what he had discovered that he ran out into the street crying "Eureka!" (which is Greek for "I have found it!").

What Archimedes had found was that an object immersed in water displaces its own volume of water.

Archimedes

Archimedes was a mathematician, engineer, and scientist from ancient Greece. He lived in Syracuse on the island of Sicily. In mathematics, he found new methods of measuring areas and volumes, and developed ways of dealing with very large numbers. He invented a pump that used a rotating, angled screw for lifting water, and made pulley blocks for lifting very heavy weights. But he is best known for discovering Archimedes' principle, which states that the upward force on an object immersed in a liquid is equal to the weight of the liquid displaced. A Roman army attacked Syracuse in 215 B.C., and Archimedes was killed three years later by a Roman soldier.

ARCHIMEDES' PRINCIPLE

When a weight is suspended in water, it appears to weigh less by an amount equal to the weight of water displaced.

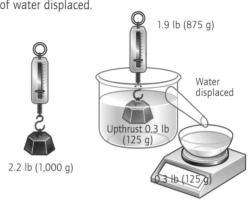

1.9 lb (875 g)

Water displaced

Upthrust 0.3 lb (125 g)

2.2 lb (1,000 g)

0.3 lb (125 g)

In addition, he also realized that the force keeping an object afloat—the so-called upthrust, or buoyant force—is equal to the weight of the water (or whatever fluid the object is floating in) it displaces. This last statement is known as Archimedes' principle. Any object that weighs more than the buoyant force will sink. But an object that weighs less than the buoyant force will float.

Another story about Archimedes shows how he put his principle to good use. Archimedes lived in the city of Syracuse on Sicily. One day the king of Syracuse asked for his help. The ruler had been given a golden crown, and he asked Archimedes if he could find out whether it was made of pure gold (without melting down the crown and destroying it). Archimedes first weighed the crown and then immersed it in a bowl of water and measured the volume of water displaced. This volume of water equaled the volume of the crown. So Archimedes divided the weight of the crown by its volume, which gave him the density of the metal. He knew the density of pure gold, and so he could tell whether the crown was or was not made of pure gold. History does not record whether the king's crown was pure gold or not!

When the air inside a hot-air balloon is heated, it becomes less dense than the air outside it, and the balloon rises into the sky.

expressed as so many tons displacement, which is the weight of water it displaces. Some modern supertankers have displacements in excess of 500,000 tons. In a similar way, airships displace their own volume when they "float" in the air. The air in a hot-air balloon is less dense than the surrounding air, which it displaces as it floats.

A submarine also has a hollow hull, but it is surrounded by tanks that can be flooded with water. On the surface, the tanks are empty, and the submarine floats. To make it submerge, water is allowed into the tanks. The vessel loses buoyancy and slowly sinks. To surface again, compressed air is used to force the water out of the tanks. The vessel becomes buoyant again and rises in the water. The principle is the same for a small submersible and for a large nuclear submarine.

SUBMARINES

A submarine sinks or rises in the water as its buoyancy changes. Letting water into the ballast tanks or forcing the water out with compressed air alters the buoyancy.

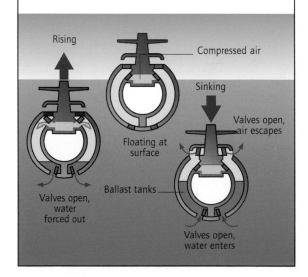

Rising
Compressed air
Sinking
Valves open, air escapes
Floating at surface
Ballast tanks
Valves open, water forced out
Valves open, water enters

Ships and submarines

Although steel is much denser than water, we can now begin to understand how a steel ship floats. A solid lump of steel always sinks in water. But the hull of a steel boat is hollow. In water, the hollow hull displaces an equal volume of water. The weight of water displaced equals the weight of the ship's hull, and so the ship floats. The weight of a ship is usually

Heat is clearly a form of energy because it can be made to do work, as it does in steam engines and gasoline engines. Hot things possess heat energy, which they "store" in their vibrating atoms or molecules. The more these particles vibrate, the hotter the material gets. Particles in cold materials do not vibrate as much.

Energy comes in many different forms. For example, light and electricity are both forms of energy. Objects in motion possess kinetic energy, and even stationary objects have potential energy. In addition, every object contains some internal energy that lies in the small vibrations of the atoms or molecules it is made of. It is this energy that we call heat. More technically, heat represents the transfer of energy from a hot object to a cooler one because of their difference in temperature.

A red-hot nail is much hotter than a bucket of warm water. Yet the water contains more heat energy than the nail. The level of "hotness" is an object's temperature, and it depends on how vigorously the object's component particles—its atoms or molecules—are vibrating. The bucket of warm water contains many more particles than the nail does, and as a result it "stores" more heat, even though its temperature is

much lower. Adding heat to an object will increase its temperature, while removing heat from it will have the opposite effect, that is lowering its temperature.

Units of heat

Because heat is a form of energy, its correct scientific unit is the joule. Technically, 1 joule is the amount of work done when a force of 1 newton acts through a distance of 1 meter. All forms of energy—and work—can be measured in joules.

An older unit called the calorie (abbreviation cal) is still sometimes used to measure heat. One calorie is the heat needed to raise the temperature of 1 gram of water through 1°C. The calorie is a small unit, and

SCIENCE WORDS

- **calorie:** (cal) A unit of heat equal to the amount of heat needed to raise the temperature of 1 gram of water through 1°C.
- **Calorie:** (with a capital C) 1,000 calories, the same as a kilocalorie.
- **joule:** (J) The SI unit of energy, equal to the amount of work done when a force of 1 newton acts through a distance of 1 meter.

A grass fire quickly gets out of control as it is spread by the wind. It is an example of the potential destructive power of flames.

often the kilocalorie is used in practice. One kilocalorie (kcal) equals 1000 calories. To add to the confusion, dieticians who deal with the energy values of foods call this unit the Calorie (with a capital C); 1 Calorie equals 1,000 calories. Often the capital C is omitted on food labels. So a 200-calorie piece of candy actually has an energy content of 200 kcal—more than enough to boil 2 kg (just over 2 quarts) of water.

Sometimes it is necessary to convert calories into joules (or vice versa). You need to know that 1 calorie equals about 4.2 joules (4.1868 joules, to be precise).

TRY THIS

Warmer is wetter
Warm water is "thinner" than cold water, and as a result it flows more easily. Here is a simple demonstration that this is so.

What to do
Wash out two paper cups thoroughly if they have been used. Turn the cups upside-down, and in the center of the base of each make a small hole with a pin. Carefully fill one cup about three-fourths full with very hot water from the hot-water faucet and set it on top of a glass. Put the same amount of cold water in the other cup, add an ice cube, and set it on top of another glass. Now watch what happens.

The hot water will drip out faster than the cold water. This is because it is "thinner"—in scientific terms it is less viscous (a very viscous liquid is thick, like syrup). The molecules of the hot water move much more quickly than those in the cold water. For this reason, they slip past one another—and through holes—more easily. If you have ever had leaky faucets in your home, have you noticed that the hot faucet nearly always leaks more than the cold faucet? Now you know why.

Hot water drips through a small hole quicker than cold water does.

21

PRODUCING HEAT

Heat can be produced in many ways—by burning things, by using electricity, even by rubbing your hands together. You can also feel heat in the Sun's rays, while the Earth's core is a source of heat, which can be tapped to generate geothermal power. Nuclear reactors also produce heat.

Because heat is a type of energy, it is generally produced by converting other forms of energy. For example, when a piece of coal burns, the chemical energy in it is released as heat in the chemical reaction called combustion (burning). Chemical energy is converted to heat when any fuel burns and is often put to use in heat engines such as the diesel engine in a truck.

Another source of heat for homes and industry is electricity. Electric heaters rely on the fact that when an electric current flows through a piece of wire, the wire gets hot. Special high-resistance wire is used so that it does not burn away or get too hot and melt.

Mechanical energy into heat

The conversion of mechanical energy into heat was observed in the 1790s by Count Rumford (1753–1814). He correctly assumed that the mechanical energy of a machine boring a cannon barrel was converted to heat because of friction between the drill and the metal of the barrel. He even submerged the barrel and the drill in a tank of water, and after a while the water in the tank boiled because of the heat produced.

HEAT PRODUCTION

Six sources of heat are combustion (burning), electricity, the Sun, friction, geothermal (from the center of the Earth), and a nuclear reactor.

Combustion (burning)

Electrical heating

Solar heat

Friction (car tire spinning)

Geothermal (volcano)

Nuclear (power plant)

The back tires of a drag racer spin at the beginning of a run. Friction makes the surface of the tires so hot that they burn as the car streaks away.

Heat caused by friction creates major problems in any kind of machinery that has moving parts. Engineers design special bearings for rotating shafts to minimize friction, which can also be reduced by using a lubricant such as oil. Also, many drilling and milling machines employ a watery lubricating liquid that flows over the workpiece and carries away the heat produced.

Other sources of heat

Various natural objects are hot and can give up some of their heat. Such objects include the Sun, whose heat you can feel with your skin, and the Earth itself. The Earth's core, at a temperature of about 7200°F (about 4000°C), is surrounded by a 1,850-mile (3,000-km) thick mantle of molten rock, topped by a rocky crust. By drilling down into the crust (which is up to 25 miles/40 km thick), engineers can tap the Earth's internal heat. Hot springs and volcanoes also bring this geothermal energy to the surface.

Count Rumford

Count Rumford was born Benjamin Thompson in 1753 in Woburn, Massachusetts. The son of a farmer, he became an international politician and physicist. He spied for the British during the War of the American Revolution and in 1775 went to England before moving on to Germany, where he became a count. Watching machines boring cannon barrels at the Munich arsenal, Rumford noticed how hot they got. He realized that heat is a form of energy produced by friction. After his return to England in 1798, he invented several devices, including a kitchen stove, an oil lamp, and a photometer (for measuring the brightness of light).

We all know that something with a high temperature is hot. So temperature is the degree of the hotness of something, which is a measure of how vigorously its atoms or molecules are vibrating. Scientists express temperatures on a temperature scale.

We know that if we want to make something hotter, we have to supply it with heat. It would be very useful if we could take a hot object, put it in contact with a warm one, and have heat travel from the warm object

TEMPERATURE SCALES

The chief temperature scales are the Fahrenheit scale, used for weather forecasts and everyday purposes; the Celsius scale (formerly called centigrade), used in science and for everyday measurements in most European countries; and the Kelvin scale, which is based on absolute zero. A Kelvin degree is the same size as a Celsius degree.

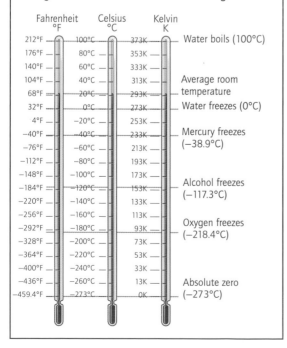

Fahrenheit °F	Celsius °C	Kelvin K	
212°F	100°C	373K	Water boils (100°C)
176°F	80°C	353K	
140°F	60°C	333K	
104°F	40°C	313K	Average room
68°F	20°C	293K	temperature
32°F	0°C	273K	Water freezes (0°C)
4°F	−20°C	253K	
−40°F	−40°C	233K	Mercury freezes
−76°F	−60°C	213K	(−38.9°C)
−112°F	−80°C	193K	
−148°F	−100°C	173K	
−184°F	−120°C	153K	Alcohol freezes
−220°F	−140°C	133K	(−117.3°C)
−256°F	−160°C	113K	
−292°F	−180°C	93K	Oxygen freezes
−328°F	−200°C	73K	(−218.4°C)
−364°F	−220°C	53K	
−400°F	−240°C	33K	
−436°F	−260°C	13K	Absolute zero
−459.4°F	−273°C	0K	(−273°C)

to the hot one—making it even hotter. But this goes against the laws of physics. One of these laws states that heat will not flow of its own accord from a cool object to a warmer one, only from warm to cooler. If we get too hot in the summer, we cool down by moving to somewhere that is colder—such as a swimming pool.

Scales of temperature

To measure an object's temperature we use some form of thermometer (see left). The thermometer has to be

Temperatures in blast furnaces reach 3600°F to 4200°F (2000 to 2300°C). Here, a worker in a steel mill pours out molten metal.

thermometer in 1709, invented the Fahrenheit scale. On this scale, the freezing point of water is 32°F, and the boiling point is 212°F. The Celsius scale was devised by the Swedish astronomer Anders Celsius (1701-1744) in 1742. It has the freezing point of water as 0°C and the boiling point as 100°C. Since there are 100 degrees in this range, it was originally called the centigrade scale ("centi-" meaning a hundred).

Another way to consider temperature is as thermodynamic temperature, based on the motion of atoms and molecules. The lowest temperature possible is called absolute zero, which equals -273°C (-459.4°F). At this temperature atoms and molecules stop moving altogether, so nothing can be made any colder. Scientists measure thermodynamic temperature on the Kelvin scale, on which absolute zero is 0 K (notice there is no degree sign). On this scale, the freezing point of water (0°C) is 273 K. A Kelvin degree is the same size as a Celsius degree. Temperature differences—as opposed to fixed temperatures—are often expressed in Kelvin rather than Celsius. The scale is named after the Scottish physicist William Thomson (1824-1907), who became Lord Kelvin in 1892 when he was knighted for his services to science.

graduated in degrees of hotness. These graduations together form a temperature scale, and over the years various scales have been devised. Most have to have at least two fixed points, such as the temperatures at which water freezes and boils.

Two common temperature scales are named after their inventors. The German physicist Gabriel Fahrenheit (1686-1736), who made the first alcohol-containing

SCIENCE WORDS

- **Absolute temperature scale:** The temperature scale that begins at absolute zero. It is also called the Kelvin temperature scale.
- **Celsius scale:** A temperature scale that has 100 degrees between the freezing point of water (0°C) and the boiling point of water (100°C). It used to be called the centigrade scale.
- **Centigrade scale:** An old name for the Celsius scale.
- **Fahrenheit scale:** A temperature scale that has 180 degrees between the freezing point of water (32°F) and the boiling point of water (212°F).

It takes a certain amount of heat to raise the temperature of water to its boiling point. But you have to keep on supplying heat to boiling water to convert it into steam. This extra heat is called latent heat.

Whenever a solid melts to form a liquid, or a liquid boils to form a gas or vapor, we say that a change of state occurs. Similar changes happen when a gas or vapor condenses to form a liquid, or when a liquid freezes to form a solid.

Every change of state involves the absorption or release of heat. It takes heat to melt ice—not just to raise its temperature but to change it from a solid to a liquid. This heat is called latent heat, and for ice it takes 80 kcal to melt 1 kg (2.2 lb). Its temperature remains at 0°C—freezing point—all the time. (This is one area where kilocalories are generally used instead of joules for measuring heat.) Thus we say that the latent heat of fusion of ice is 80 kcal/kg. Not surprisingly, the latent heat of freezing of water is

Once the water in a kettle is boiling, supplying more heat turns the boiling water into steam. This is latent heat of vaporization.

exactly the same. You have to remove 80 kcal from 1 kg of water in order to convert it into ice.

The latent heat of vaporization also applies to the change from liquid to gas or vapor. For water, it has a value of 540 kcal/kg: it takes 540 kcal to change 1 kg of liquid water at 100°C into 1 kg of steam at the same temperature. The latent heat of condensation, the amount of heat that must be removed to convert 1 kg of steam at 100°C to 1 kg of liquid water at 100°C, is also 540 kcal. When a liquid evaporates, it takes heat from its surroundings. That is why sweating makes you cooler. The latent heat of vaporization of the watery sweat is removed from your skin.

Solid to vapor

Some solids are unusual because when they are heated they turn directly into a vapor without melting first. This process is given the name sublimation, and the solid is said to sublime. It occurs because the boiling point of the solid is actually less than its melting point at atmospheric pressure. Examples of substances that sublime are solid carbon dioxide ("dry ice") and iodine. At any temperature above –109°F (–78.3°C), solid carbon dioxide changes directly into a gas.

Carbon dioxide and iodine sublime at ordinary atmospheric pressure. Other solids can be made to sublime by greatly reducing the pressure on them. This is the principle of the freeze-drying process for foods and instant coffee. The food is frozen at very low pressure so that the ice sublimes out of it to leave behind a dehydrated product. Conversely, at high pressures a substance that sublimes at atmospheric pressure can be made to melt in the usual way. Liquid carbon dioxide can be produced at high pressures.

SCIENCE WORDS

● **Latent heat:** The heat taken in or given out when a substance undergoes a change of state. The latent heat of fusion is the heat needed to change a solid at its melting point into a liquid (and is the same as the latent heat of freezing). The latent heat of vaporization is the heat needed to change a liquid at its boiling point into a vapor (and is the same as the latent heat of condensation).
● **Vaporization:** The change from liquid to gas or vapor on heating.

HIDDEN HEAT

The word "latent" means "hidden," and this diagram shows where the hidden heat goes. First, it takes 80 kcal (80,000 calories) to melt 1 kg of ice supplied with heat at the rate of 10 kilocalories per minute. Then, when the water has been heated to its boiling point, it takes another 540 kcal to turn 1 kg of water into 1 kg of steam.

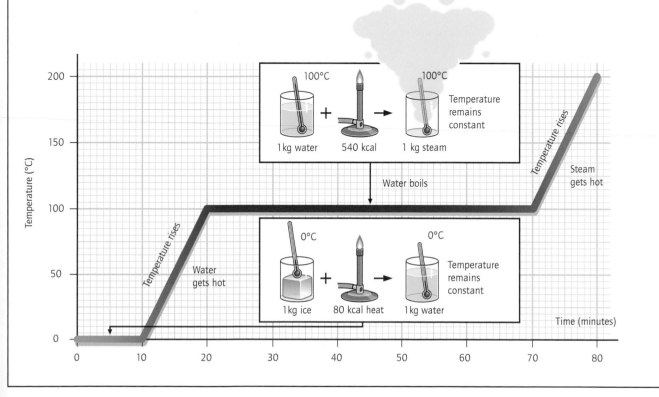

EXPANSION OF FLUIDS

To a physicist, a fluid is any gas or liquid, such as air, steam, or water. These two states of matter are grouped together because they share a common property: they can both flow—hence the name. Fluids also share another property: they expand when they are heated. This property is employed in thermometers of various kinds.

EXPANSION OF MERCURY

A teaspoonful of mercury equals about 5 ml (milliliters), which is the volume of mercury in a large laboratory thermometer. The illustration shows how much this volume of mercury expands when heated to 50°C and to 100°C.

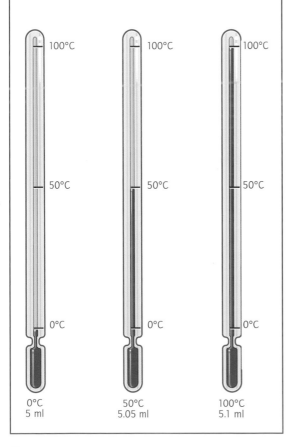

0°C	50°C	100°C
5 ml	5.05 ml	5.1 ml

Liquids or gases have no definite shape—they take up the shape of the vessel containing them. For these, we can therefore consider only volume expansion. (Of course, making a liquid expand along a narrow tube, as in a thermometer, has the effect of producing what appears to be linear expansion—along a line, as shown in the illustration below left.)

For a liquid, expansion is measured as its coefficient of volume expansion (also called volume expansivity). This is the proportion by which the original volume expands when the temperature is increased by 1 K. These coefficients are very small, but still up to ten times larger than those for solids, and they vary slightly depending on the temperature at which they are measured. For example, water has a coefficient of volume expansion of 0.0003 per K, while that of mercury is even smaller at 0.000018 per K. Mathematically, the coefficient is equal to the increase in volume divided by the original volume per degree K rise in temperature.

Measuring liquid expansion

It is straightforward to define the coefficient of volume expansion of a liquid—we have just done so. But it is quite another matter to try to measure it. That is because the liquid has to be held in a container of some sort, and any attempt to measure its expansion on heating has to take into account the fact that the container will expand as well.

This difficulty can be demonstrated by making a mark on the side of a glass beaker level with the surface of a liquid. When the beaker is heated (from below), the level of the liquid falls at first as the beaker expands. Then, as the heat reaches the liquid, it too expands, and its level rises above the mark. As a result, we can only measure the apparent expansion of the liquid. For this reason, physicists sometimes distinguish between a liquid's absolute (or true) coefficient of

The expansion of hot gases is what propels a shell out of a gun, demonstrated here by a tank firing its cannon.

TRY THIS

Climbing water
In this project, you will make a liquid expand and climb vertically up a tube.

What to do
Place a bottle top, flat part upward, on a stone or concrete surface (or use a brick). Using a hammer and nail, make a hole in the center of the top. You may want to get an adult to help with doing this. Push a drinking straw through the hole in the bottle top. If the hole is not big enough, gently enlarge it by turning the blades of a pair of closed scissors in the hole. Again, an adult could help. Push a straw down far enough that it nearly touches the bottom of the bottle when the top is screwed on. Pack modeling clay around the straw to seal the hole in the bottle top.

Half-fill a bottle with very cold water containing a little food coloring. Set the bottle inside a bucket or bowl. Use a jug to fill the bucket with hot water from the hot-water faucet to the same level as the colored water in the bottle. Watch what happens.

As the colored water in the bottle is heated by the hot water in the bucket, the colored water expands. Because the top end of the drinking straw is open, the colored water moves up the straw. It may even get right to the top and form a miniature colored fountain. Movement of a warmed liquid along a tube in this way is how an ordinary thermometer works.

The colored water rises up the tube and may even spill out as a miniature fountain.

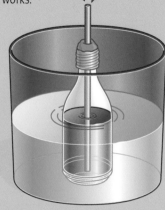

expansion and its apparent coefficient of expansion. There are ways of getting around this difficulty if we know the coefficient of volume expansion of the material of the beaker, in this case glass.

Exceptional water

In the same way that ice is a very unusual solid because it expands as it cools, water is also exceptional in the way that it behaves. When cold water is warmed from a temperature of 32°F to 39.2°F (0°C to 4°C), it takes up less volume—it contracts. Above 39.2°F (4°C) it begins to expand, behaving in the same way as most other liquids.

Also, because density equals mass divided by volume, and warming does not change the mass of water, water must be at its densest at about 39.2°F (4°C). This effect has some extremely important consequences for fish. Since water near the surface of a lake cools toward the freezing point in winter, its

density increases, and it sinks to the bottom. Eventually the surface water reaches a temperature of 39.2°F (4°C); but then, as it cools further, the colder water remains at the top—because it is less dense than the water lower down. Even when the surface freezes over and forms ice, the water at the bottom remains liquid at a temperature of 39.2°F (4°C), so providing a safe home for fish.

CHARLES'S LAW

The volume of a gas increases by 1/273 of its volume at 0°C for every degree Celsius rise in temperature. Therefore a balloon with a volume of 10 cu m at 0°C increases in volume to 15 cu m at 137°C and doubles in volume to 20 cu m at 273°C.

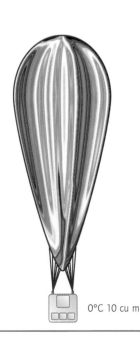

0°C 10 cu m

137°C 15 cu m

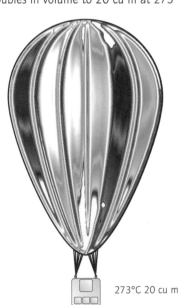

273°C 20 cu m

Expansion of gases

Heating increases the volume of a gas as long as its pressure is kept the same. Like a liquid, a gas therefore has a coefficient of volume expansion defined as the increase in volume of 1 cu cm of a gas at 0°C for a rise in temperature of 1 K (at constant pressure). It turns out to have the same value for all gases and is equal to 0.00366 per degree K. This is equal to the fraction 1/273, as predicted by Charles's law. The law states that at constant pressure the volume of a given mass of gas increases by 1/273 of its volume at 0°C for every degree Kelvin rise in temperature. As a result, the volume of a gas at a constant pressure is proportional to its absolute temperature: that is, its temperature on the Kelvin temperature scale (remember that degrees Kelvin equals degrees Celsius plus 273).

Gases have another coefficient of expansion, which is measured in terms of changes in gas pressure when the volume is kept constant. It is called the pressure coefficient and turns out to be equal to 0.00366 per K (or 1/273 per K), the same as the volume coefficient.

This fact should come as no surprise because both coefficients represent the effect of heating on the molecules. At constant pressure, the molecules acquire more energy and move farther apart and so increase the volume. At constant volume, the more energetic molecules collide with the walls of the container more frequently and thus increase the pressure.

Putting gases to work

The pressure created by heating a gas can be made to do work. For example, gas pressure is used in steam engines, internal combustion engines (gasoline and diesel), gas turbines, and pneumatic tools. Hot expanding gases are also the propellants in rockets and guns. Balloons also contain gas. In a hot-air balloon, air is heated so that it expands and becomes less dense than the surrounding air, making the balloon rise. Expansion caused by heating also has to be taken into account with gas-filled balloons, as explained in the illustrations on page 30.

TRY THIS

The dime that dances

Heat makes solids, liquids, and gases expand (get bigger). This project illustrates a strange effect produced by expanding air.

What to do

Place a dime over the top of a bottle. Dip your finger into some water and drip a little around the edge of the coin to act as a seal. Grip the bottle in both hands for about 20 seconds (being careful not to dislodge the dime). The dime will start to move up and down, making a clicking sound. Keep hold of the bottle for a while, then put it down. The dime will go on dancing.

When you grip the bottle, the heat of your hands warms the air inside the bottle. The warmth makes the air expand, and it has to push past the dime to escape from the bottle. The dime goes on dancing until the air pressure inside the bottle is the same as the air pressure outside it.

Escaping warm air makes the dime dance a jig on the top of the bottle.

BOILING AND EVAPORATION

When a liquid is heated above a certain temperature, it boils and turns into a gas, usually called a vapor. Steam is the gas formed when water boils. Liquids also turn to vapor when they evaporate, even though they are not boiling.

The molecules in a liquid are free to move around, allowing a liquid to flow and take up the shape of its container. When the liquid is heated, the extra energy makes the molecules move ever faster and move farther apart. Eventually, at a certain temperature called the boiling point, the molecules are so far apart that they become a gas. Usually the gas first forms within the liquid near the base of the container that is being heated. It takes the form of bubbles, which move rapidly upward and make the liquid froth. Boiling is complete when the bubbles reach the surface and burst.

Different liquids boil at different temperatures. The boiling point of water, for example, is 212°F (100°C), while that of ether is only 94°F (34.5°C). That is so low that a drop of ether will boil if placed on the palm of your hand. The liquid metal mercury does not boil until it reaches about 676°F (358°C). That makes it a good liquid to use in thermometers. The metal tungsten, which is used to make electric lamp filaments, has the highest boiling point of all. It boils at the incredible temperature of 10,220°F (5660°C), which is as high as the temperature at the surface of the Sun.

Changing boiling point

Various things can alter the boiling point of a liquid. A liquid boils when the pressure of the gas inside the bubbles is the same as atmospheric pressure—the pressure of the air at the surface of the liquid. If we change the pressure, the boiling point changes. For instance, the air pressure at the top of a high

LEAPING WATER MOLECULES

In a boiling liquid (a), high-energy "hot" molecules leap out of the surface and form bubbles of vapor in the liquid. In evaporation (b), high-energy molecules leave the surface of the liquid even though it is not heated. As a result (c), the liquid loses heat energy, and it gets cooler.

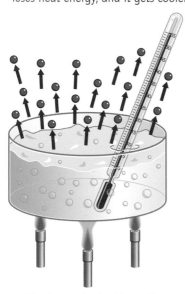

(a) Boiling: molecules driven off

(b) Evaporation: molecules escape

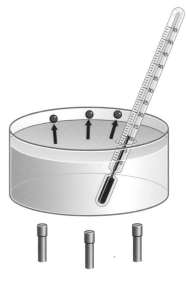

(c) Evaporation causes cooling

mountain is much less than it is at sea level. As a result, water boils at a lower temperature at the mountaintop. For example, at an altitude of about 10,000 ft (about 3,000 meters) water boils at 194°F (90°C). Mountaineers say that it is very difficult to make a good cup of coffee at the top of a mountain—because the pressure is lower, the water does not get hot enough.

The 18th-century American scientist Benjamin Franklin (1706-1790) once did a simple experiment that demonstrated the effect of pressure on boiling point. He heated water in a flask until the water boiled, then sealed the flask with a cork. The water soon cooled slightly, and boiling stopped. He then

An erupting hot spring or geyser is an impressive sight. Below the geyser, groundwater flows down a channel in the rock, to where the underground rocks are very hot. The heat boils the water, which forms steam. The pressure builds up until the steam explodes back up the channel, taking with it any water in its way.

turned the flask upside down and poured cold water over it. Some of the steam above the water in the flask condensed, making the pressure inside the flask less than the atmospheric pressure outside it. As a result, the water started to boil again.

On the other hand, increasing the pressure on a liquid makes it boil at a higher temperature. This principle is used in an autoclave for sterilizing surgical instruments and in a pressure cooker for cooking food. If the pressure in the cooker rises to twice the atmospheric pressure, the boiling water is at a temperature of 248°F (120°C). As a result, the food cooks much quicker—potatoes cook in less than half the usual time. At 15 times the atmospheric pressure, water does not boil until the temperature reaches 392°F (200°C).

The boiling point of a liquid also depends on its purity. An impure liquid boils at a higher temperature than a pure liquid. That is why adding salt to water raises its boiling point: potatoes cook quicker in boiling water with salt added. How much the boiling point rises depends on the concentration of the added

SCIENCE WORDS

- **Atmospheric pressure:** The pressure of the Earth's atmosphere at any point on its surface (caused by the weight of the column of air above it). Atmospheric pressure decreases with altitude.
- **Boiling point:** The temperature at which a liquid changes into a gas or vapor.
- **Condensation:** The process by which a gas or vapor changes into a liquid. The liquid formed is also sometimes called condensation.

THE WATER CYCLE

The water cycle describes how the Earth's water goes around and around, alternating mainly between the clouds and the oceans and rivers. In fact, 97.3 percent of the water is always in the oceans, with only 0.014 percent in lakes and rivers. Clouds account for even less—about 0.001 percent. Most of the remainder is locked up as ice in the north and south polar ice caps and in glaciers.

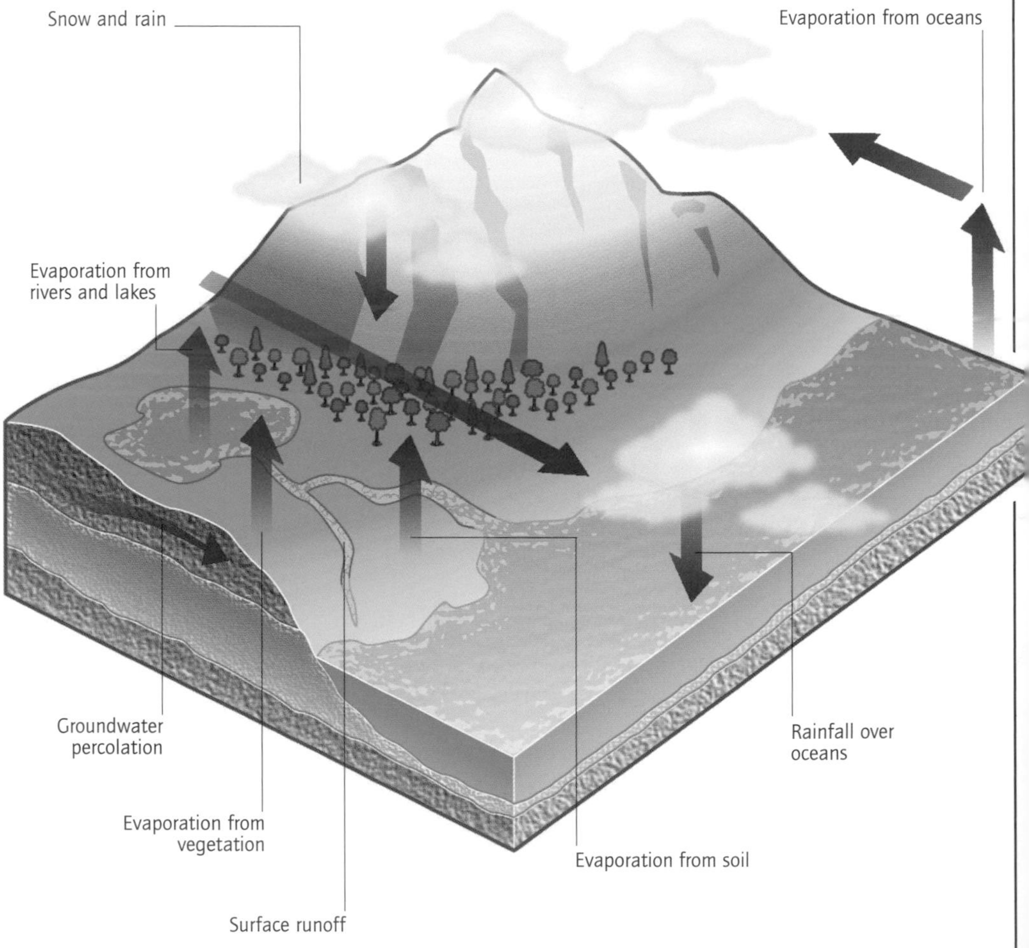

Snow and rain

Evaporation from oceans

Evaporation from rivers and lakes

Groundwater percolation

Evaporation from vegetation

Surface runoff

Evaporation from soil

Rainfall over oceans

substance. Chemists measure the rise in boiling point to find the concentration of a solution and can even use such measurements to calculate the molecular weight of the substance that is dissolved.

Low-temperature vaporization

In boiling, heat makes a liquid turn to gas or vapor. But vapor can form without heat being applied. A puddle formed after it has rained gradually dries up. Where does the water go? It turns to vapor. We know that the molecules in a liquid move around. At the surface of the liquid, some of the faster molecules leap right out of the surface, become vapor, and do not return. The name of this process is evaporation. It can happen at any temperature but gets faster as the temperature rises.

The faster molecules leaving the surface during evaporation take heat energy with them. As a result, the liquid that remains gets cooler. That is why laundry hung out to dry gets cold as the water evaporates from it. And it accounts for the cooling effect of sweating. When a human or other animal sweats, the liquid perspiration evaporates, taking heat with it.

A simple device for keeping drinks cool works by the same principle (see "Try This" right). It consists of a porous pot, such as an unglazed flowerpot. It is soaked in water and placed over the drink, such as a carton of milk or a can of soda. As the water evaporates from the pot, it removes heat and keeps the drink cool. Some wine bottle coolers work in the same way.

Water goes around and around

Everyone knows that rainwater comes from clouds. But how did the rain get there? It all depends on the evaporation of water from rivers, lakes, and seas. It rises into the sky as water vapor, where it cools and condenses into tiny droplets of water. The living processes of plants also give off water vapor, adding to the vapor in the sky. Clouds can be blown around by the wind, but eventually the water droplets get large enough to fall as rain. If it is cold enough, it falls as snow.

TRY THIS

Keeping your cool
How can you keep a cold drink cool in the summer if you do not have an icebox? One way is to apply a scientific method that has been in use for hundreds of years.

What to do
Soak a clay pot in a bucket of water overnight. The next day, pour some cold water into a bowl, place a drink bottle in it, and cover it with the upside-down flowerpot. Put a small stone over the hole in the base of the pot. The drink will stay cool.

What happens is that water evaporates from the surface of the pot. As it does so, it draws heat from its surroundings. Because the pot is porous, it soaks up water from the bowl like a sponge, keeping the pot wet so that evaporation keeps on going. Of course, you will have to taste the drink from time to time just to make sure it is keeping cool!

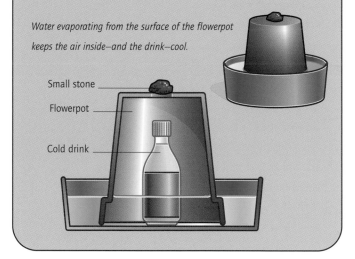

Water evaporating from the surface of the flowerpot keeps the air inside—and the drink—cool.

Small stone

Flowerpot

Cold drink

Most melted snow and rainwater forms streams and rivers that eventually flow back to the sea. Some evaporates from the ground. Other water soaks into the ground and may reemerge in springs. And some of the groundwater is taken up by plants and passed back into the air from their leaves as water vapor. The whole circuit is called the water cycle.

EXPANSION OF SOLIDS

When a solid is heated, the atoms or molecules of which it is composed vibrate more vigorously. Because these particles vibrate more, they take up more room. As a result, the solid gets bigger—it expands. And the more you heat it, the larger it gets.

Expansion of solids—particularly metals—can be a problem. It can cause steel railroad lines to buckle and concrete roads to crack. In the Middle East, high daytime temperatures cause oil pipelines to lengthen, meaning they would buckle if the pipes did not include expansion loops. Even overhead power lines can droop dangerously low when the cables expand in summer.

But like most other phenomena in physics, the expansion of solids has also been put to good use. For example, some types of thermometers and thermostats rely upon the difference in expansion between two different metals bonded together (a bimetallic strip). Some, such as a gas control valve, are illustrated here, but first we should understand why expansion occurs.

Metal girders on bridges expand when it gets warm in summer. These roller bearings allow the bridge to move without structural damage.

EXPANDING METALS

Different metals expand by different amounts when they are heated. The diagram shows the amount of expansion when 5-meter lengths are heated through 90°F (50°C).

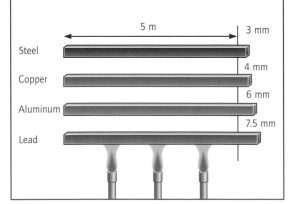

5 m

Steel — 3 mm
Copper — 4 mm
Aluminum — 6 mm
Lead — 7.5 mm

Moving molecules

All solids are made up of atoms and molecules. These particles are in a constant state of motion—after all, their vibrations are what defines heat. Add more heat, and they vibrate more vigorously (and the temperature of the solid rises). One consequence of this extra molecular motion is that the solid expands. A long bridge may expand by 3 feet or more (around 1 meter) when it heats up in summer. The actual amount of expansion will depend on what the bridge is made of. Steel, for example, usually expands more than concrete.

Measuring expansion

A scientific measure of how much a solid increases in length when heated is its coefficient of linear

expansion (also called expansivity). It is defined as the proportion by which its original length increases when its temperature rises through 1 K. The coefficient of linear expansion is very small for most solids, varying from only 0.0000005 per K for the glassy substance quartz to 0.000024 per K for the metal lead. What these figures mean in real terms is shown opposite.

Heated solids also increase their volume, so they have in addition a coefficient of volume expansion (just like liquids and gases). Think of a cube. When it is heated, each of its three dimensions increases. It is therefore not surprising that the coefficient of volume expansion is usually three times the value of the coefficient of linear expansion.

GAS CONTROL VALVE

When the valve is open, it admits gas to an oven's burners. As the oven heats up, a brass tube in the oven expands and lengthens. This action pulls a rod of Invar (an alloy that does not expand when heated) and closes the valve to reduce the gas flow.

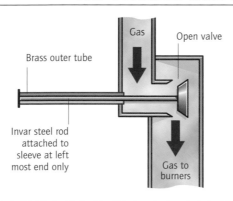

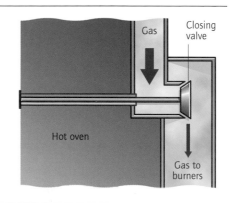

SOLIDS INTO LIQUIDS

The molecules or atoms in a solid remain in a regular arrangement, which is what gives a solid its shape and hardness. But what happens if we supply heat energy to a solid? It melts.

The effect of heat on a solid's molecules is to make them vibrate faster. Eventually they break away from their regular positions and move about freely, just as in a liquid. In fact, the solid has become a liquid—it has melted. Every pure solid undergoes this change at a definite temperature, called its melting point.

The melting points of different substances span a wide range of temperatures. Ice is a familiar solid—it is the solid form of water. It melts at 32°F (0°C), and its melting point is used as the lower fixed point on the Celsius temperature scale. The metal mercury, on the other hand, melts at about –38°F (–39°C). That is why mercury is liquid at ordinary temperatures. Tungsten melts at the very high temperature of 6170°F (3410°C). It is used to make the filaments of electric light bulbs. In fact, there are very few things that will not melt if they are made hot enough—even rocks and concrete will eventually melt.

Changing melting points

We saw on pages 32–35 how decreasing the pressure on a liquid lowers its boiling point. Pressure can also affect the melting point of a solid, although a lot of pressure is required to make much difference. The British physicist John Tyndall (1820-1893) once devised a simple experiment to demonstrate this effect. He took a large block of ice (which is a solid) and supported it between two chairs. He then attached heavy weights to each end of a thin steel wire, and hung the wire around the ice block. The wire exerted a great pressure on the ice immediately under it, and the ice melted to form liquid water. The wire sank a little way into the water before the ice refroze above it. In this way, with alternate melting and freezing, the wire gradually cut its way right through the block of ice.

We make snowballs by taking a handful of snow and squeezing it. The pressure melts some of the snow, which refreezes when the pressure is released, leaving a hard ball of snow. If the snow is too cold, we cannot squeeze hard enough to melt it, and it is difficult or impossible to make snowballs.

A stream of molten lava flows down the side of a volcano. The rocks deep underground take the form of magma, which is kept liquid by intense heat and comes to the surface as lava when volcanoes erupt.

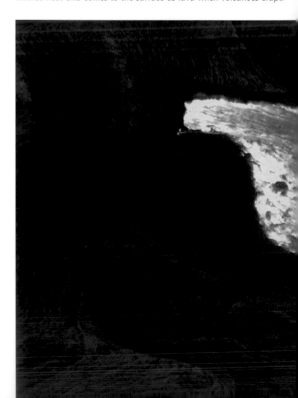

MELTING MOLECULES

When a solid is heated, its molecules move faster and away from their regular positions in the solid. Order changes into disorder. Eventually the solid melts and becomes a liquid.

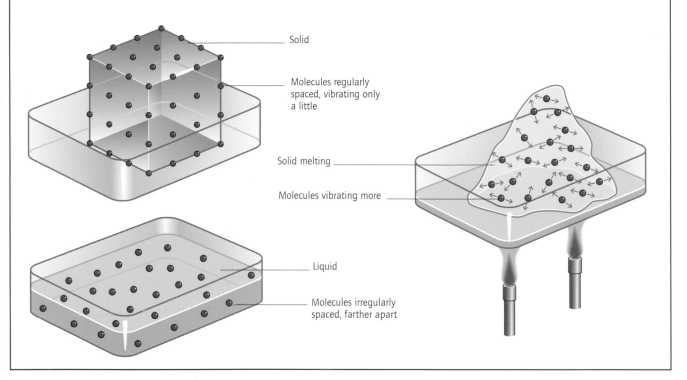

Solid

Molecules regularly spaced, vibrating only a little

Solid melting

Molecules vibrating more

Liquid

Molecules irregularly spaced, farther apart

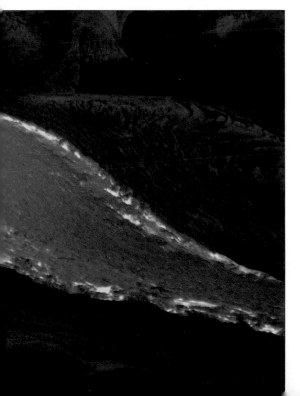

Most solids expand on melting because their molecules are farther apart in the liquid state. This effect is put to good use in a device for automatically opening the windows in a room or greenhouse when the temperature rises to a certain point. The device consists of a cylinder of wax with a tight-fitting piston. As the temperature rises and the wax melts, it expands. This moves the piston, whose movement opens a window.

The chemical naphthalene also expands when it melts. A clever device for keeping a constant temperature makes use of this property. A coil of wire carrying an electric current inside a can of naphthalene gets warm and begins to melt the naphthalene. The expanding chemical presses a spring-loaded switch, which cuts off the electricity to the heating coil. So the naphthalene cools and solidifies again. The switch restores the current, and the action is repeated over and over.

The handle of a metal spoon left in a hot drink quickly warms up and may get too hot to hold. Heat travels along the spoon by conduction. But not all materials conduct heat as well as metals do. Very poor conductors of heat are called insulators.

We all know that heat can travel easily through some substances. But others do not conduct heat very well—the handle of a plastic spoon hardly gets warm if

---

THREE WAYS THAT HEAT TRAVELS

If you put a metal rod in a pan of hot water, heat travels up the rod by conduction. Convection makes currents of water circulate from the heated bottom of the pan, and heat also escapes from the electric stove by means of radiation. These are the three ways that heat can travel.

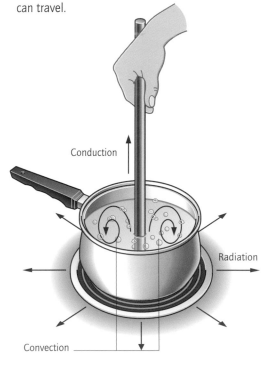

Conduction

Radiation

Convection

---

the spoon is left in a hot drink. So how does heat travel in this way, and why are metals better heat conductors than plastics are?

As with many other phenomena in physics, to answer these questions we have to take a look at the atomic or molecular structure of the materials. A metal is made up of regularly spaced atoms that vibrate slightly around their usual positions. A "sea" of what are called free electrons occupies the spaces between the atoms.

When a substance is heated, its atoms vibrate more vigorously. The atoms at the hot end of a heated bar are the ones that vibrate the most. As they do so, they bump into their neighbors, increasing the neighbors' rate of vibration. Increased vibration means higher temperature. In this way, the vibrations gradually increase along the length of the spoon, and this is how heat travels from the hot end toward the cool end. The atoms themselves do not move from their average positions. In a metal bar, free electrons moving rapidly along it carry most of the heat.

The internal structure of a plastic spoon is quite different. Plastics are composed of large molecules with no free electrons between them. The molecules do vibrate, and a similar ripple effect does conduct some heat along the spoon. But the process is very slow.

We therefore say that metals are good conductors of heat, while nonmetals such as wood and plastics are poor conductors, or insulators. A saucepan is made of metal so that it will rapidly conduct heat from a stove to the pan's contents. But it has a wooden or plastic handle that does not get too hot for you to hold.

As well as heat, materials also conduct electricity. There are good electrical conductors and there are poor electrical conductors, which are also known as insulators. As with heat, most good conductors of electricity are metals, while nonmetals make up most of the poor conductors. This similarity is no coincidence.

Both kinds of conduction depend to some extent on the same property of the material—the number of free electrons available in its structure. With electricity the free electrons carry current through the material. And

with heat the "hot" free electrons have a high kinetic energy, which they carry through the material to the colder part before giving it up in collisions with atoms. Insulators—both electrical and heat insulators—do not have free electrons to fulfill these functions.

Rate of heat flow

Several things affect the rate at which heat is conducted by a substance. Consider a block of material with one end being heated. The rate of heat flow through the block depends on its length. The longer it is, the more slowly heat flows from one end to the other. The cross-sectional area of the block also matters—the greater this area, the faster heat will flow. The difference in temperature between the two ends of the block is also obviously important. The greater this difference, the faster heat will flow.

The temperature of a furnace has to be in excess of 1650°F (900°C) to soften glass. The rod held by the glassblower is made of a poor heat conductor, so he does not burn his hands.

SCIENCE WORDS

- **Conduction:** The process by which heat moves through a solid object. (In electricity conduction is the process by which an electric current moves through a substance.)
- **Electron:** A subatomic particle with a negative electric charge. Electrons surround the nucleus of an atom.
- **Kinetic energy:** The energy an object possesses because it is moving.

Finally, there is a property of the material itself that is a measure of how well it conducts heat. It is the material's thermal conductivity. When heat is measured in joules, the units of thermal conductivity are watts per

TRY THIS

Heat on the move

Heat moves through solids by the process called conduction. But some solids conduct heat better than others. In this project, you will see how well or badly three different solids conduct heat.

What to do

Stand a metal spoon, a plastic spoon, and a wooden spoon upright in a mug or bowl. Use a small blob of margarine or butter to stick a bead near the top of each spoon. Carefully pour very hot water into the mug and watch what happens.

Heat from the hot water gradually moves along the spoons. When the heat gets near the end of a spoon, it melts the margarine, and the bead drops off. The first bead to drop off indicates the spoon that is the best conductor of heat. Which spoon was it? Which was next? You should find that metal is a better conductor of heat than either of the nonmetals. Poor conductors of heat are called heat insulators. Can you think of anything else that metals conduct better than nonmetals?

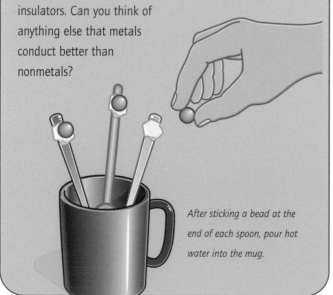

After sticking a bead at the end of each spoon, pour hot water into the mug.

meter per K. The chart on page 44 compares the thermal conductivities of various substances. Silver is the best heat conductor of all, while the poorest are feathers and the vegetable fiber kapok. That is why these sorts of materials are used for heat insulation in bed covers and padded winter clothing.

Notice that cork is a particularly poor conductor. You can feel this for yourself if you compare walking in bare feet on a ceramic tiled floor and walking on a floor covered with cork tiles. Cork feels much warmer because it does not easily conduct the heat away from your feet. For a similar reason, glass wool is used for insulating lofts and for wrapping water pipes to prevent them from freezing in winter.

Solid plastic foams, also called expanded plastics, are very poor heat conductors (or good heat insulators). A common example is expanded polystyrene (Styrofoam). You can hold a Styrofoam cup containing a hot drink: that is because the plastic does not conduct the heat to your fingers. Foam plastics are sometimes pumped into the cavity walls of buildings. This makes the building cool in summer (by keeping the Sun's heat out) and warm in winter (by stopping internal heat from escaping through the walls).

Conduction by fluids

Heat can also travel through fluids—liquids and gases—by conduction, although this is not the usual way heat travels in such substances. Air has a thermal conductivity of 0.025 watts per meter per K, which is about the same as the conductivity of feathers. This means that air is a very poor conductor or, put another way, a very good heat insulator. It explains why furs and loosely knitted clothing keep you warm in winter. The air trapped in the materials acts as an additional insulator.

Convection of heat

Heat normally travels through a fluid—a gas or a liquid—by convection. In this process the material itself actually moves (which is why it cannot take place in solids). When a hot fluid moves, it takes heat with it

Polar bears' fur keeps them warm in their Arctic habitat. Fur is a very poor conductor of heat and so is a good insulator against the cold.

and displaces any cold fluid in its way. Also, cold fluid moves in to take the place of the rising hot fluid. In this way the fluid circulates by creating a convection current.

The hot fluid is less dense than the cold fluid that surrounds it. As a result, it is more buoyant and tends to rise. Such natural convection currents have various uses. Soaring birds such as eagles make use of updrafts of warm air, called thermals, to fly effortlessly. Pilots of gliders and hang gliders also make use of thermals to keep their aircraft flying without the use of motors.

Effect on the weather

Large-scale convection currents in the atmosphere play a major part in creating and controlling the weather. As the air near the ground becomes warmer, it retains water vapor because warm air can hold more moisture than cold air can. Eventually the warm air rises, carrying the water vapor with it. But when this air

HOW HEAT TRAVELS

Heat travels through a solid by conduction. Imagine that the solid bar in this illustration has its lower end in a fire. The atoms at this hot end vibrate vigorously. These "hot" atoms joggle their neighbors, and they in turn joggle their neighbors, but not quite so much. The middle of the bar gets warm. Only at the cold end do the atoms vibrate normally. In a metal, heat is conducted mainly by free electrons moving between the atoms.

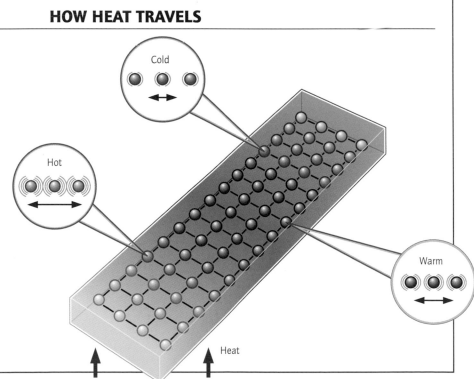

meets the colder air above, it can no longer hold all the water vapor, which condenses out as tiny droplets of water. These masses of droplets are clouds, in this case the type of cloud called cumulus.

Convection currents also give rise to winds and breezes. Near a seacoast in summer, during the day the land warms up more quickly than the sea. The warm air above the land rises, cools, and then sinks down again over the sea. This sets up a circulating convection current with a gentle wind blowing onshore off the sea, called a sea breeze. The situation is reversed at night, when the land cools down more rapidly than the sea. The result is a land breeze, blowing out to sea.

Liquid convection

Warm water can also transfer heat by convection, and for the same reason. The warm water is less dense than surrounding colder water, and it rises, setting up a convection current. The principle is used in some hot-water heating systems in homes and offices. Hot water from a boiler rises and enters a cylindrical hot-water tank, where it transfers its heat to water circulating around the radiators.

On a much larger scale, convection takes place in the world's oceans. Water near the equator is warmer and less dense than the water nearer the poles. It tends to stay close to the surface and is displaced by colder water from polar regions. The deep-water currents that result shift huge volumes of water. Between Greenland and Iceland, for example, 1 billion gallons (5 million cu m) of water flows into the North Atlantic every second. This type of flow should not be confused with currents like the Gulf Stream, which are a surface effect caused mainly by the wind.

GOOD AND BAD CONDUCTORS

Thermal conductivities of common materials (in watts per meter per degree K). You can see why feathers and kapok make good insulators to line padded clothing.

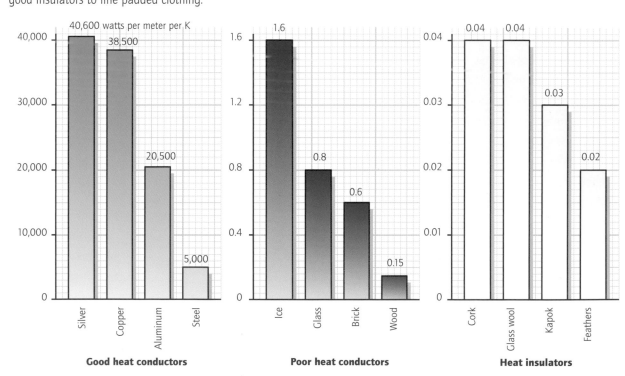

CLOUD FORMATION

Convection currents can cause clouds to form. Warm air, heated by the land, can hold more water vapor than cold air can. Convection makes this warm air rise, where the water vapor cools and condenses out as clouds of water droplets.

Warm air

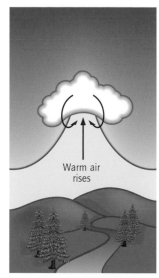

Warm air rises

Forced convection

Even when there are no density differences that will set up natural convection, blowers (for air) and pumps (for water) can circulate fluids to transfer heat. A hot-air heating system has fans to blow air heated by a furnace along ducts to each room. In a car's cooling system, a pump circulates cooling water between the engine and the radiator.

Heat radiation

We will now consider a method of heat transfer that needs no medium in which to travel—radiation.

In radiation, energy travels as electromagnetic waves. There are many kinds of these waves, including gamma rays, x-rays, microwaves, and radio waves. The most familiar are the waves of visible light—which enable us to see—and their invisible companions, ultraviolet light and infrared radiation. They all have different wavelengths, and they all travel at the speed of light.

Cumulus clouds (from the Latin word for "mass") form by the process described in the diagram above. The process requires the land to be warm, so such clouds are usually an indication of good weather.

The waves that mainly concern us here, infrared radiation, possess wavelengths that are slightly longer than the wavelengths of visible light.

Any object whose temperature is above absolute zero gives off infrared radiation. In other words, every normal object emits some infrared. But the hotter the object, the more infrared it emits. You cannot see the radiation from a hot radiator in a room, but you can feel it if you carefully place your hand near the radiator. In fact, another name for infrared is heat radiation. All the heat radiated by the Sun is in the form of infrared.

Detecting radiation

Scientists use various instruments and techniques to detect electromagnetic radiation. Electronic circuits connected to an antenna can detect microwaves and radio waves.

Gamma rays, x-rays, and visible light can be detected by photographic film, as in a camera or an x-ray machine. Special film can also detect ultraviolet light and infrared radiation, while astronomers use various electronic devices to study such radiations that are emitted by heavenly bodies.

Alternatively, infrared radiation can be measured using a device called a thermograph. It produces a picture of a hot object, with the temperatures of various areas represented as different colors or shades of gray.

In a solar oven, a giant mirror focuses heat radiation from the Sun. It provides a source of cheap and clean heat for heating water and cooking. Large solar furnaces are used for melting metals.

Thermographs are used in medicine, for example, for diagnosing tumors. The skin over a tumor is slightly warmer than the skin around it and shows up as a light area on a thermograph.

Heat and color

Infrared radiation comes from a hot object's vibrating atoms or molecules. The more they vibrate, the more radiation they emit. But increasing the vibration of an object's atoms also increases its temperature. It

SCIENCE WORDS

- **Convection:** The usual way in which heat moves through a fluid (a liquid or gas) by setting up convection currents in the fluid.
- **Convection current:** Movement of a fluid (a liquid or gas) that results when warm fluid rises and cold fluid flows in to take its place.
- **Thermal:** A vertical convection current in a gas, usually air.
- **Thermal conductivity:** A measure of the ability of a substance to conduct heat.

therefore follows that the amount of infrared radiation an object emits increases as its temperature rises.

The wavelength of the radiation also depends on the temperature of the emitting object. The higher the temperature (i.e., the greater the vibration), the shorter the wavelength. When an object is heated, it begins to emit more infrared. Then, as its gets hotter, it becomes red. At this stage, its temperature is about 1110-1300°F (600-700°C). When it is even hotter, it turns orange (1750°F/950°C), then yellow (2000°F/1,100°C), and finally it becomes white hot at a temperature of about 2550°F (1400°C). It is now emitting white light as well as infrared radiation. In this way, it is possible to estimate a hot object's temperature merely from its color, which is a skill used by blacksmiths and others who deal with very hot metals, and also by astronomers studying the stars.

Although infrared radiation is invisible to the human eye, scientists can make photographic film and television camera tubes that are sensitive to infrared. They have many practical uses. For example, infrared cameras on orbiting Earth satellites, such as the *Landsat* series, take infrared pictures of crops and other vegetation on which damaged or diseased plants show up differently from healthy ones.

Harnessing radiant energy

Our largest source of radiant energy—mainly light and infrared radiation—is without doubt the Sun. It lies at the great distance of 93 million miles (150 million km), and it emits radiation in all directions across the vacuum of interplanetary space. On the daylight side of the Earth, radiant energy from the Sun arrives at a rate of 1.4 kilowatts per square meter (kW per m^2). One way of capturing some of this free energy is to use a large curved mirror to focus the Sun's radiation in a solar furnace. This radiation can also make electricity in solar cells, although they are expensive and not very efficient converters of energy. They tend to be reserved for spacecraft, where they last much longer than any battery would.

TRY THIS

Underwater fountain
On the bottom of the deep oceans, there are underwater fountains called black smokers. They occur where hot liquids escape from cracks in the Earth's crust and rise into the cold water of the sea bottom. In this project, you will make your own underwater fountain.

What to do
Fill a bucket nearly to the top with cold water (or you could use the kitchen sink). Put a couple of marbles in a bottle to weight it down (any other small heavy objects would do, such as a couple of steel nuts). Fill the bottle to the top with hot water, and add several drops of food coloring. Cover the top of the bottle with plastic film, and secure it with the rubber band. Now stand the bottle at the bottom of the bucket of cold water. When the water has become still, take a pencil and make a small hole in the plastic film with the point of the pencil, taking care to disturb the water as little as possible. Carefully remove the pencil, and watch what happens.

The hot colored water is less dense than the cold water (because the hot water molecules are moving faster and taking up more room). As a result, the hot water rises, just as a cork or piece of wood bobs up to the surface of water. The process is called convection and is what happens with the undersea black smokers.

Use two marbles to weight down a small bottle of colored hot water. Put it in a bucket of cold water and watch what happens.

RADIATORS AND ABSORBERS

Have you noticed that in warm weather you feel cooler in a white T-shirt than in a dark-colored one? Things that are black or dark-colored absorb heat better than things that are white or shiny. Black things are also better at emitting heat radiation.

Everything emits some radiation, as explained from pages 45 to 47. Some things are better than others at emitting heat radiation. In general, black surfaces are good emitters—much better than surfaces that are white or shiny. That is why a hot drink stays hot longer in a shiny metal mug than in a dark-colored china cup.

In addition, good emitters are good absorbers of heat radiation. The best absorber of all is a theoretical object called a black body, which absorbs all radiation falling on it. It is also the best emitter. Nobody has been able to make a perfect black body, but a mat black surface comes very close to perfection. For this reason, a car's radiator is generally painted mat black

James Dewar

James Dewar was a Scottish scientist who lived and worked mainly in London. He is best known for inventing the vacuum bottle, or Dewar flask (described opposite), in the early 1870s. He used his flasks during his researches into cryogenics (low temperatures), and by the year 1899 he had developed a large-scale method for liquefying hydrogen at a temperature of –423°F (–253°C). A year later, he produced solid hydrogen at –434°F (–259°C). In chemistry, in 1889 with Frederick Abel (1827–1902) he invented the propellant explosive cordite (based on guncotton), the first so-called smokeless powder. He also worked on specific heat capacities and on using the spectra of metallic elements as a means of identifying them. In 1904 he was knighted by King Edward VII.

so that it emits the heat from the water circulating inside it. Solar panels on houses are thin tanks containing water. They are also painted mat black, but this time in order to absorb as much of the Sun's heat radiation as possible to heat the water, which is then pumped into the house.

Stopping heat losses

A common need, both in science and in everyday life, is to prevent hot liquids from cooling down or cold liquids from warming up. The second of these problems faced the Scottish scientist James Dewar (1842–1923) when he was dealing with liquid gases such as liquid nitrogen, which boils at –320.4°F (–195.8°C). His solution was the Dewar flask, or vacuum bottle, which we still use today, although mostly for keeping hot drinks hot.

The vacuum bottle (also called a thermos bottle) works because it prevents the three methods of heat transfer—conduction, convection, and radiation. It consists of two thin-walled glass bottles, one inside the other, with all the air removed from the space between them. This vacuum prevents heat from traveling by conduction because there is nothing for the heat to travel in. It also prevents heat from being transferred by convection because there is no fluid to circulate and carry the heat (see diagram opposite).

In addition, the glass walls of the double bottle are covered with a layer of silver, like a mirror. This silvered surface minimizes heat loss by radiation because shiny objects are very poor emitters of radiant heat.

Trapping heat

When an object absorbs heat radiation, it becomes hotter than its surroundings. But any object that is hotter than its surroundings gives off heat. The heat emitted has a longer wavelength than the heat

The tremendous heat produced by the Sun travels across space as infrared radiation. You can feel the loss of this heat when the Sun goes behind a cloud.

absorbed. This fact is put to good effect in a greenhouse, which traps heat.

The soil and plants inside a greenhouse absorb radiation from the sunlight that passes through the glass, making them warmer. They then reradiate the heat as longer-wavelength infrared radiation. But these longer waves cannot pass through glass, and as a result the heat is trapped inside the greenhouse. The temperature inside is up to 15 to 20°C (27 to 36°F) warmer than the outside.

VACUUM BOTTLE

The vacuum bottle, or Dewar flask, is designed to prevent the loss of heat by all the processes described in the illustration on page 40. The vacuum prevents heat loss by conduction or convection, and the silver mirror minimizes loss through radiation. The stopper prevents heat loss through evaporation.

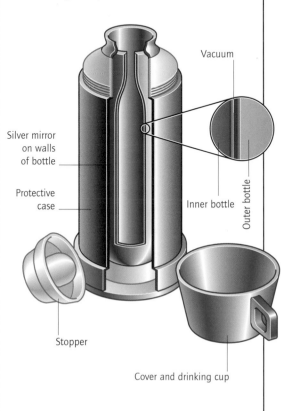

Silver mirror on walls of bottle

Protective case

Vacuum

Inner bottle

Outer bottle

Stopper

Cover and drinking cup

EFFECTS OF COOLING

Here we will look at how cooling affects the arrangement of atoms and molecules.

Cooling a substance has the effect of slowing down the movement of atoms and molecules. When a gas is cooled, its molecules move more slowly and do not travel so far. This has the effect of reducing the pressure of the gas. If it is made even cooler, the molecules begin to behave like those in a liquid. The gas (or vapor) will have condensed into a liquid. That is what happens to the steam coming from the spout of a kettle of boiling water. In the cooler air, the steam condenses to form tiny droplets of water. They are the white "steam" that we see; like clouds in the sky, steam consists of water droplets.

As a gas cools, its volume decreases. In fact, at constant pressure all gases "shrink" by 1/273 of their volume at 0°C for every degree Celsius fall in temperature. This relationship between the volume of a gas and temperature is called Charles's law, after Jacques Charles (1746-1823), the French scientist who discovered it (also see the illustration on page 30). It is usually stated in this form: the volume of a fixed mass of gas at constant pressure is proportional to its

(also see the illustration on page 30)

SCIENCE WORDS

- **Condensation:** The process by which a gas or vapor changes into a liquid. The liquid formed is also sometimes called condensation.
- **Superconductor:** A substance that shows no resistance to the passage of electric current; some metals do this when cooled close to absolute zero (–273.15°C/–459.67°F).

absolute temperature. Absolute temperature is Celsius temperature plus 273, so you can see where the fraction 1/273 comes from.

Liquid gases

If the pressure on a gas is increased sufficiently, it turns into a liquid. Or at least this is true of many gases. There are some, however, that have to be cooled as well as being put under pressure before they will liquefy. The temperature below which they must be cooled is called the critical temperature. For example, carbon dioxide gas cannot be liquefied by pressure alone unless it is cooled below 88.3°F (31.3°C), which is its critical temperature.

COOLING SEQUENCE

The effect of cooling on the states of matter is illustrated here. Cool a gas sufficiently, and it condenses into a liquid. Cool a liquid, and it eventually freezes to form a solid.

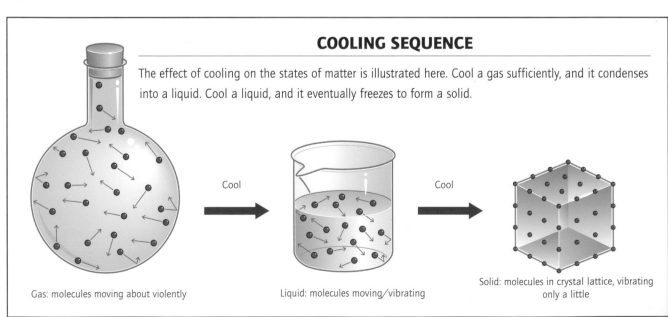

Cool

Cool

Gas: molecules moving about violently

Liquid: molecules moving/vibrating

Solid: molecules in crystal lattice, vibrating only a little

Some gases have to be made extremely cold indeed to liquefy them. At ordinary pressure, oxygen liquefies at –297.4°F (–183°C), and liquid nitrogen forms at –320.4°F (–195.8°C). Liquid air also has a temperature of about –321°F (–196°C).

Liquefied gases, such as liquid helium (which is the coldest), are used to surround and cool large computer memories and also big magnets used in medical scanning machines. Liquid hydrogen is used as a rocket fuel, and liquid nitrogen is employed as a refrigerant and for liquefying natural gas.

Cooling liquids

If cooling a gas turns it into a liquid, cooling a liquid turns it into a solid. The temperature at which this occurs is called the freezing point of the liquid. It is exactly the same as the melting point of the solid.

Sometimes you can cool a liquid below its melting point without it freezing. This is called supercooling. If the temperature of the supercooled liquid rises slightly, the solid and liquid forms exist together for a while until the whole lot solidifies.

Cooling solids

As a liquid cools, it slowly crystallizes to form a solid. The nature of the crystals depends on how fast the liquid cools. If it cools rapidly, only small crystals have time to form. But if the liquid cools very slowly, there is time for large crystals to grow. These effects are best seen with minerals, large crystals of which form only if cooling has been slow.

Most solids shrink in size as they get colder, but ice actually expands, by as much as 10 percent. This can have disastrous effects on water pipes and the engine blocks of automobiles, which may burst if the water in them freezes. But it does mean that ice is less dense than water, which is why it floats. This is important for fish and other aquatic creatures in winter. Ice forms as a layer on the surface of a pond or river, so the fish remain unfrozen in the warmer water beneath. Metals may also have unusual properties at low temperatures.

TRY THIS

Lifting the ice
This project can be made into a puzzle. How can you lift a cube of ice without touching it with your fingers? Simple—make it even colder!

What to do
Float an ice cube on the surface of some water in a glass. Lay one end of a piece of string across the top of the ice cube, and sprinkle salt on the string. Wait half a minute and gently lift the string. The ice cube will be frozen onto the string and can be lifted with it.

Pure water freezes at a temperature of 32°F (0°C). But salt water freezes at a much lower temperature—which is why it has to be very cold indeed for the sea to freeze. When you sprinkle salt on the string lying on the top of the cube, you lower the freezing point. At first, the ice melts a little, but the coldness of the ice cube then causes the salt water to freeze again, locking the string onto the cube as if it were glued on.

Sprinkle the string with salt to make it stick to the ice cube.

The crystal structure of some metals changes. The crystals grow larger, and the metal loses strength, becoming brittle and snapping easily. At very low temperatures, close to absolute zero, some metals lose their electrical resistance. There seems to be nothing to stem the flow of electricity through them, and they become what are called superconductors. Researchers continue to search for materials that are superconductors at higher temperatures.

PRESSURE ON GASES

A gas is the one state of matter that can be compressed—increase the pressure on a gas, and its volume gets smaller. This can be an extremely useful property.

Compressing a gas requires an input of energy. The resulting compressed gas is therefore a store of energy that is capable of doing work. Scientists and engineers have devised many ways of using the energy of gases under pressure. It is important to remember that, scientifically, a vapor is a gas. Common vapors include steam and the mixture of gasoline and air that provides the source of energy in an automobile engine.

Compressing gases

To make use of compressed gases, we must either compress them where we use them or store the gases under pressure for use somewhere else. The gas that is

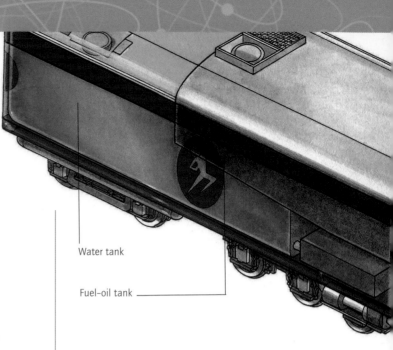

Water tank

Fuel-oil tank

The tender, pulled behind the locomotive, carries a supply of water and fuel—in this case fuel oil. The hot gases produced by burning oil in the firebox pass along tubes inside the boiler. The water surrounding these firetubes boils and produces steam. The steam is led to the cylinders before being vented up the chimney. This makes a draft, which pulls hot gases and smoke through the boiler's firetubes. Connecting rods and cranks make the back-and-forth movement of the pistons turn the driving wheels.

most commonly employed in the latter way is compressed air. It is produced by a machine called—not surprisingly—a compressor. Most compressors consist of an engine or a motor that works a piston. The piston moves rapidly back and forth in a cylinder to compress air, which is stored in a strong metal tank or in cast-iron bottles called cylinders.

Cylinders of compressed air have many uses, from blowing up balloons for a party to working a spraygun for repainting an automobile. You may have seen portable compressors on trailers where workers are breaking up the concrete of roads or old buildings. The jackhammers they use are powered by compressed air.

Another type of compressor has a rotary motion and works a bit like a water pump. The fastest types are equipped with blades like the blades of a turbine. Every jet engine has a compressor like this to compress the air for burning the vaporized fuel in the engine.

SIMPLE AIR COMPRESSOR

A bicycle pump is an air compressor. When the handle is pulled back (a), air moves past the piston into the barrel. When the handle is pushed in (b), the piston fits tightly and compresses the air.

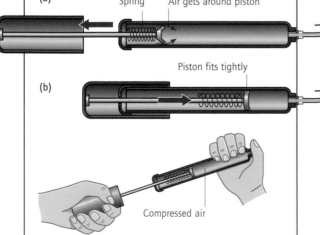

(a)   Spring   Air gets around piston

Piston fits tightly

(b)

Compressed air

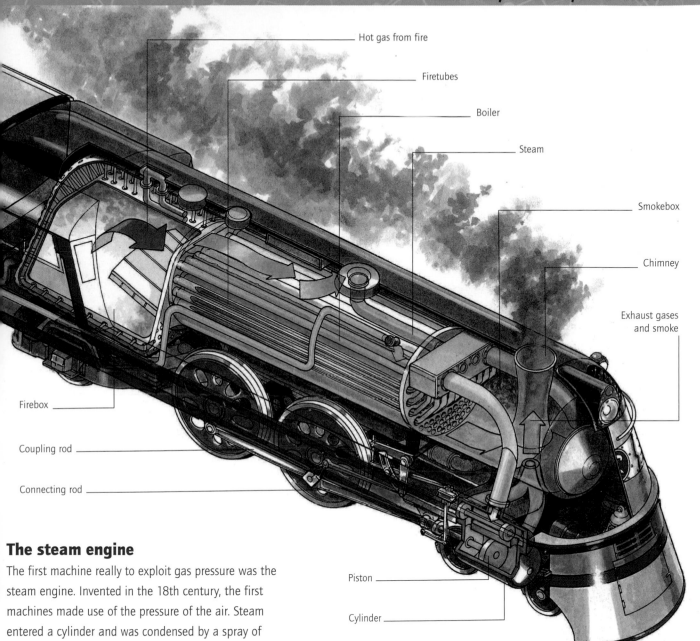

Hot gas from fire

Firetubes

Boiler

Steam

Smokebox

Chimney

Exhaust gases
and smoke

Firebox

Coupling rod

Connecting rod

Piston

Cylinder

The steam engine

The first machine really to exploit gas pressure was the steam engine. Invented in the 18th century, the first machines made use of the pressure of the air. Steam entered a cylinder and was condensed by a spray of cold water. This left a partial vacuum in the cylinder, and atmospheric pressure then pushed down a piston. These machines were therefore known as atmospheric engines. Soon the Scottish engineer James Watt (1736–1819) started building engines that used the pressure of steam to move the piston, and that remained the basic principle of all steam engines.

Steam engines introduced the Industrial Revolution. Stationary steam engines drove spinning machines and looms in textile factories, and portable engines on wheels were employed for plowing. Steam engines

powered boats, road carriages, and eventually locomotives for railroads. From about 1830 to 1930, steam power was the main type of traction on the world's railroads. Steam locomotives are now mainly seen only on heritage lines.

The key parts of a steam locomotive are a fire, which heats a boiler for making steam, and a cylinder mechanism that uses steam pressure to produce motion. The fuel for the fire may be wood, coal, or oil. The heat from the fire passes along tubes that run the length of the boiler and are surrounded by water. The boiler is therefore called a firetube boiler. The steam, now under high pressure, moves a piston back and forth in the cylinders. Systems of valves open and close to let the steam into the cylinders, and out again when it has done its work. The waste steam passes up a chimney, along with the smoke from the fire.

The internal combustion engine

In a steam engine, the fuel is burned outside the engine itself—it is an external combustion engine. Toward the end of the 19th century, inventors in Germany and elsewhere began to make engines that burned fuel inside them—they were internal combustion engines. The earliest type used flammable gas, such as coal gas, and later a mixture of gasoline and air, as fuel. It was exploded inside the cylinders of the engine, and the rapidly expanding hot gas moved the pistons within the cylinders. An electric spark from a sparkplug ignited the gasoline vapor. This is still the principle on which most of the world's automobile engines work.

The German engineer Rudolf Diesel (1858-1913) invented another type of internal combustion engine. But in the diesel engine, as it came to be called, the compression of the vaporized fuel is enough to make it explode—there is no need for sparkplugs. From its way of working it is also known as a compression–ignition engine. Diesel engines are commonly used in trucks, railroad locomotives, and automobiles.

A jackhammer is powered by compressed air. The air is released in rapid bursts, causing a piston to hit the top end of the cutting chisel. It is not a new idea. A French engineer invented it in 1861 for drilling the first tunnel through the Alps between France and Italy.

SCIENCE WORDS

- **Compressor:** A machine for compressing a gas (that is, putting a gas under high pressure).
- **Partial vacuum:** A region of low atmospheric pressure, especially one in which most of the air has been pumped out.
- **Vapor:** Another name for the gas that forms when a liquid boils or evaporates.

There is a third type of internal combustion engine that has no pistons at all. It uses the hot gases from burning fuel to turn the blades of a turbine and for this reason is called a gas-turbine engine. The blades of a compressor are mounted on the same shaft as the turbine blades. It is located in front of the turbine, and its job is to compress air for feeding into the combustion chamber. When they are first started, these engines need an electric motor to spin the shaft and get the compressor working before fuel is injected and ignited.

A jet of hot gases leaves the rear of the engine, giving it its more common name—the jet engine. There are various types, used for both military and civil aircraft.

Gas-turbine engines power some modern high-speed railroad locomotives. They are also used in small power plants (to drive electricity generators) and as standby engines in large power plants for use in the event of a steam-turbine breakdown.

Propellant gases

Similar in some ways to jet engines are rocket engines. They too burn fuel in a combustion chamber, and the resulting hot gases expand through a nozzle at the rear and create the thrust to push the rocket along.

But it is not the jet of hot gases pushing against the air that creates the thrust of a rocket engine. It is the reaction force against the front of the combustion chamber that gives the forward "push." For this reason, rocket engines are normally known scientifically as reaction motors.

All the internal combustion engines just described—and steam engines—use the oxygen in the air to burn their fuel. A rocket is different because it carries its own oxygen supply. A liquid-fueled rocket, such as the giant Saturn V employed to launch the American Apollo Moon shots, has tanks of liquid oxygen and liquid hydrogen as fuel. Solid-fueled rockets, as their name suggests, burn a solid fuel. The simplest of them burns gunpowder, like the rockets used as fireworks. It takes time to prepare a liquid-fueled rocket for launching, but solid-fueled rockets are ready to use right away. They power military missiles and act as launch boosters for larger rockets. And because they have their own supply of oxygen, all rockets work in the airless conditions of outer space.

Explosives that push shells and bullets out of the barrel of a gun are similar to solid rocket fuel. The firing pin of the gun detonates a small charge in the base of the cartridge, which in turn explodes the main charge. The large volumes of hot expanding gases produced push the bullet rapidly out of the barrel.

TRY THIS

Crush a bottle
A simple of way to demonstrate the air pressure around us is to use atmospheric pressure to crush a bottle.

What to do
Unscrew the cap from an empty plastic drink bottle and carefully pour in about half a cupful of hot water from the faucet. Let the bottle stand for a couple of minutes, and then pour out the water. Quickly screw the cap on tightly, and watch what happens. It is as if an invisible pair of hands is slowly squeezing the bottle.

After you screw on the cap, the bottle cools. As it cools, hot water vapor inside the bottle condenses and forms small droplets of water. They take up far less room than the water vapor, but no air can enter the bottle to fill up the vacated space. As a result, a partial vacuum forms inside the bottle. The pressure of the air outside the bottle then crushes it (because there is not enough air inside to push back). Normally, even an empty bottle is full of something—it is full of air.

Let the bottle and the hot water in it stand for a couple of minutes before you tightly screw on the cap.

PRESSURE ON LIQUIDS

Unlike gases, liquids cannot be compressed. This means that pressure applied at one place in a liquid is transmitted immediately to every other part of it. This important principle is used in hydraulic machinery, from large presses for stamping out automobile bodies to bulldozers and backhoes.

The molecules in a gas are relatively far apart. When we apply pressure to a gas, the molecules are squeezed closer together, and the volume of gas gets smaller. But the molecules in a liquid cannot be squeezed any closer together. As a result, a liquid cannot be compressed. Applying pressure can, however, move a liquid. This is what a pump does. The pump on a fire truck produces a jet of water that can reach the roof of a building.

Pressure units

Pressure is a force acting over an area. It is equal to the total force divided by the area concerned. The scientific unit of pressure is the pascal, named after a French physicist who studied the subject. In customary units, pressure is usually given in lb per sq in (which is sometimes abbreviated to psi). A single lb per sq in is equal to nearly 7,000 pascals.

There are various other pressure units. The millibar is used in weather forecasting to express the pressure of the atmosphere. One millibar equals 100 pascals. The word "atmosphere" is also the name for a unit of pressure. It is equal to the average pressure of the Earth's atmosphere at sea level and is about 100,000 pascals or 14.7 lb per sq in.

Hydraulic press

A hydraulic press has two pistons: a small one and a large one, connected by a pipe (see upper diagram on page 57). The arrangement is filled with an oily liquid. Because pressure is transmitted equally throughout a liquid, a small force on the small piston results in a greater force on the large piston. For example, if the large piston has ten times the area of the small piston, a weight of 2.2 lb (1 kg) placed on the small piston will

To reach the top of a building on fire, the water in a firefighter's hose has to be at high pressure. A pump in the fire truck provides the pressure.

raise a weight of 22 lb (10 kg) placed on the large piston.

However, the large piston will move up only a tenth as far as the small piston moves down. For this reason, a practical hydraulic press has an arrangement of valves that allow the small piston to be pumped down repeatedly to raise a heavy weight. A common application is in the braking system of automobiles and trucks. When the driver presses on the brake pedal, it pushes a piston in what is called a master cylinder. Pipes connect this cylinder with slave cylinders at each wheel. Hydraulic fluid in the pipes transmits the pressure to the slaves, where the movement of their pistons applies the brakes. Because of the magnifying effect of using small and large cylinders, a fairly small force from the driver's foot creates a large force to apply the brakes.

Many other machines make use of hydraulic pressure, such as dump trucks, bulldozers, and even large airplanes, which employ hydraulics to operate the undercarriage and wing flaps. Most of them do not rely on the movement of a piston in a small cylinder to create the fluid pressure. Instead, they use rotary pumps to pressurize the hydraulic fluid, which is routed by a system of valves.

HYDRAULIC PRESS

Pressing down on the small piston makes the large piston move up. The pressure is the same on both pistons, but the force is not the same. A small force on the small piston creates a large force on the large piston.

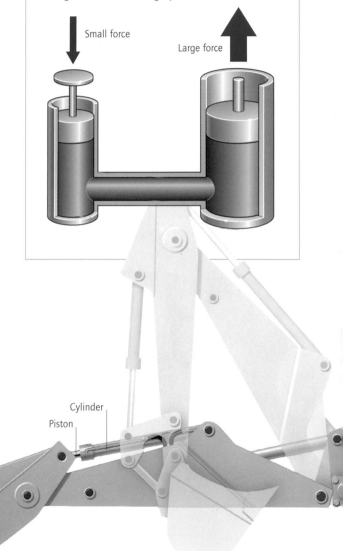

All the movements in the arm and bucket of a backhoe are produced by hydraulics. Notice the piston-and-cylinder arrangement at each of the pivots. A pump pressurizes the fluid inside the pistons and in the pipework connecting them.

FLOWING FLUIDS

We have seen on earlier pages many of the differences between gases and liquids. But in some respects they can be alike, and scientists then use the single word "fluid" to stand for both gases and liquids. Here we look at flowing fluids.

Many engineers need to know about the way things move through fluids. A speedboat slicing through the water, a jet plane flying through the air, and a supersonic bullet speeding to its target all have to be designed to push their way through a fluid. But it is difficult to study objects moving through fluids. Instead, engineers usually observe the fluid flowing past the object. The results are much the same.

All surfaces that make contact with each other experience friction, and objects moving in fluids are no exception. Friction opposes the movement, so it has the effect of slowing down a moving object. It also generates heat. A bullet is very hot when it reaches its target, and the surface of a meteorite burns away through friction when it arrives from space and plunges into the Earth's atmosphere at many miles per second.

One way of reducing the effect of friction on fast-moving objects is to design their shape so that friction is reduced to a minimum. A rifle bullet is the best shape for the job. Round bullets or square ones would not travel straight through the air—they would tumble about and probably miss their target. A normal bullet shape is streamlined, and streamlining accounts for the shapes of ship's hulls and high-speed airplanes. In the natural world many fish (such as sharks) and birds (such as swallows) also have a streamlined shape.

Smooth or turbulent?

Streamlines are the paths followed by all the particles of a fluid as they pass a particular point. It is as if the fluid consists of parallel layers—in fact, streamlined flow is also called laminar flow (from the Latin word for

The lemon shark is one of the fastest fish in the sea. Its body is perfectly streamlined so that it moves through the water effortlessly. The water nearest the shark's body moves along with it. As a result, the tiny striped pilot fish can swim along with the shark without getting left behind.

"layer"). The fluid as a whole keeps on moving smoothly in the same direction.

If an object moving in a fluid (or around which a fluid is flowing) does not have a streamlined shape, eddies and whirls begin to form in the fluid. This is called turbulent flow. It can be seen, for example, in the water at the foot of a waterfall.

Turbulence can also affect fluids flowing through pipes. That is why pipelines are made smooth on the inside with no obstructions or sharp bends. In this way the fluid flows as quickly as possible. The rate of flow equals the speed of the fluid multiplied by the cross-sectional area of the pipe. If the speed cannot be kept as fast as possible, the only way to increase the rate of flow is to make the pipe wider—a very expensive option.

Changing speed of flow

If a pipe includes a section that is narrower than the rest, the speed of flow is obviously affected. The speed increases in the narrow part, to maintain the same overall rate of flow through the whole pipe. At the same time, the pressure of the fluid falls in the narrow part. The actual pressure change can be calculated using a complicated mathematical expression called Bernoulli's equation, which also takes into account the fluid's density.

The equation makes some useful predictions about fluid pressure. It tells us that the pressure in a fluid depends on its depth. That is why a dam is built of thicker concrete near the bottom, where the pressure of water behind it is greatest. Pressure also increases with depth in the sea, for example, which is why the hulls of submarines have to be made very strong. If not, they would be crushed by the pressure.

MOVING THROUGH FLUID

When a rectangular block moves through a fluid (a), it creates much turbulence. A sphere (b) creates less turbulence, but the best shape of all is a teardrop, with no turbulence created (c).

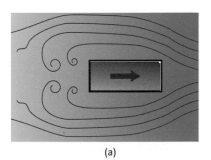

(a)

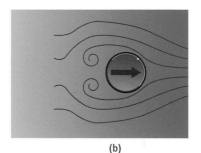

(b)

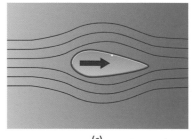

(c)

A simple experiment demonstrates this effect. Take an empty plastic drink bottle (quart or 2-liter size), and make three or four holes one above the other down one side. Put a single strip of tape over all of the holes, and fill the bottle with water. Place the bottle in the sink* and pull off the tape. The water will jet out of the holes, but which stream goes farthest? It is the one near the bottom of the bottle, where the pressure is the greatest.

There are a number of practical applications of Bernoulli's equation, which predicts that a reduction in pressure of a flowing fluid causes an increase in the speed of flow. In a chemist's Bunsen burner or in a plumber's blowtorch, for example, gas passes through a small jet before it burns at the end of a tube. This speeds up the flow of gas and lowers the pressure, which sucks in air through the holes in the sleeve around the end of the tube. The air mixes with the gas and produces a much hotter flame than if the gas burned on its own.

Drag and lift

It takes force to push an object through a fluid—jet airliners need very powerful engines. The resistance to movement is called drag, and streamlining is one way of keeping drag as low as possible. But how does an airplane fly in the first place? The answer has to do with the design of the wings.

SCIENCE WORDS

- **Airfoil:** The cross-sectional shape of an airplane wing, curved more over the top than beneath. Moving through the air, an airfoil produces lift.
- **Lift:** A force acting on a moving airfoil that keeps it in the air (because the lift is greater than the drag).
- **Turbulence:** The irregular flow of a fluid moving around an object. It is reduced by streamlining.

AIRFOIL SURFACES

The airfoil that forms an airplane's wing is slightly more curved over the top than beneath. This results in a pressure difference as the wing moves through the air, producing lift.

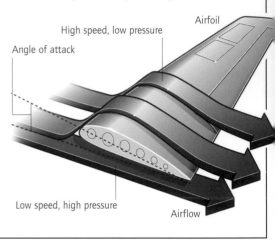

High speed, low pressure

Airfoil

Angle of attack

Low speed, high pressure

Airflow

An airplane wing is not flat. It is slightly curved in section, with more curvature on the upper surface than on the lower surface (see the diagram above). This shape is called an airfoil. As the wing moves through

A jet airliner coming in to land. Extendable flaps on the trailing edges of the wings increase the drag and decrease the stalling speed, thereby slowing the aircraft down safely as it approaches the runway.

the air, the airflow is diverted. Some air passes under the airfoil, and some flows across the upper surface. The air flowing over the top of the wing has slightly farther to go, so it has to speed up. As a result, the air pressure falls slightly (as is predicted by Bernoulli's equation). So, the air pressure is higher beneath the wing than above it. This provides an upward force called lift, and lift is what keeps the plane in the air.

To achieve maximum lift, the whole wing is angled upward slightly. The steeper the angle, the more lift is generated. This angle is called the angle of attack. But if the wing is angled too much, the airflow ceases to be streamlined. Turbulence sets in above and behind the wing. At too steep an angle there is no lift at all—the airplane stalls, and unless the pilot takes action to prevent it, the plane will fall out of the sky.

Getting it right

Ship's hulls, cars, and airplanes are all streamlined to reduce drag and thereby improve efficiency. Having to overcome drag wastes fuel. So engineers use models to test streamlining (which is very much less expensive than building a supertanker or supersonic plane to find out!). Models of ships' hulls are tested in a long narrow tank of water called a ship tank. Models of cars and planes are tested in a wind tunnel. The model is kept stationary, and air is blown past it at high speed by large fans. Smoke may be introduced into the airflow to highlight the streamlines around the model.

Bending the draft
If you blow at a piece of paper held vertically, the draft from your breath will bend the paper. If you put an obstruction between you and the paper, you would expect it to block the draft so that the paper does not bend. But it all depends on the obstruction.

What to do
Cut a strip of paper about 4 in long and ? in wide (about 10 cm long and 1.3 cm wide). Bend up one end so that it looks like a long letter "L." Use tape to fasten it to a tabletop (not on the best furniture!), as shown in the illustration. Then blow at it—it bends easily. Now place a bottle in front of the "L" to act as an obstruction, and blow at the bottle in the direction of the paper. Try blowing quickly and slowly, and try blowing softly and hard. When you get the blowing just right, the paper will bend as it did before. What has happened?

The bottle has bent the draft. That is because moving air tends to follow a curved surface. The bottle splits the draft in two and carries it around its curved sides. On the other side of the bottle the two drafts recombine and continue on, hitting the paper. That is also why you cannot always shelter from the wind by standing behind a tree—the tree trunk can bend the wind around to you.

The bottle bends the draft around its curved surface.

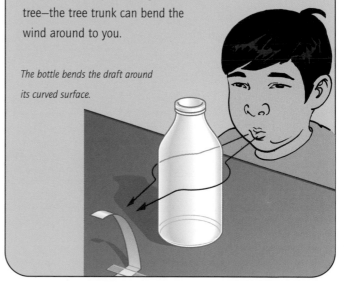

GLOSSARY

Absolute temperature scale The temperature scale that begins at absolute zero. It is also called the Kelvin temperature scale.

Airfoil The cross-sectional shape of an airplane wing, curved more over the top than beneath. Moving through the air, an airfoil produces lift.

Atmospheric pressure The pressure of the Earth's atmosphere at any point on its surface (caused by the weight of the column of air above it).

Atom The smallest part of a chemical element that can exist on its own. It has a central nucleus (made up of protons and neutrons), surrounded by electrons.

Bimetallic strip A strip consisting of two different metals bonded together. The metals have different coefficients of expansion, so the strip bends when it is heated.

Boiling point The temperature at which a liquid changes into a gas or vapor.

Boyle's law At constant temperature the pressure of a gas is inversely proportional to its volume.

calorie (cal) A unit of heat equal to the amount of heat needed to raise the temperature of 1 gram of water through 1°C.

Calorie (with a capital C) 1,000 calories, the same as a kilocalorie.

Capillarity Also called capillary action, the movement of a liquid up or down a narrow tube, caused by the attraction between its molecules and those of the tube. The surface of the liquid is curved into a meniscus.

Celsius scale A temperature scale that has 100 degrees between the freezing point of water (0°C) and the boiling point of water (100°C). It used to be called the centigrade scale in the past.

Centigrade scale An old name for the Celsius temperature scale.

Coefficient of expansion Also called expansivity, a measure of how much a substance expands when it is heated.

Coefficient of linear expansion Also called linear expansivity, a measure of how much the length of a solid object increases when it is heated.

Coefficient of volume expansion Also called volume expansivity, a measure of how much the volume of a substance (solid, liquid, or gas) increases when it is heated.

Compressor A machine for compressing a gas (that is, putting a gas under high pressure).

Condensation The process by which a gas or vapor changes into a liquid.

Condenser An apparatus for converting a gas or vapor into a liquid.

Conduction The process by which heat moves through a solid object.

Convection The usual way in which heat moves through a fluid (a liquid or gas) by setting up convection currents in the fluid.

Crystal A solid that has a regular shape because of the ordered way in which its atoms or molecules are arranged.

Density For any substance, its mass divided by its volume.

Ductile Describing a metal that can easily be drawn out to form wire.

Electron A subatomic particle with a negative electric charge. Electrons surround the nucleus of an atom.

Fahrenheit scale A temperature scale that has 180 degrees between the freezing point of water (32°F) and the boiling point of water (212°F).

Friction A force that prevents or slows down the movement of one surface against another surface.

Gas A state of matter in which the molecules move at random. A gas in a container takes on the size and shape of the container.

Geothermal energy A form of heat energy that comes from deep underground, as in geysers, hot springs, and volcanoes.

Heat The internal energy of an object that results from the vibrations of its particles (atoms or molecules).

Hydraulic press A machine that uses the pressure of a liquid to "magnify" a force.

Kinetic energy The energy an object possesses because it is moving.

Latent heat The heat taken in or given out when a substance undergoes a change of state.

Lift A force acting on a moving airfoil that keeps it in the air (because the lift is greater than the drag).

Malleable Describing a metal that can easily be beaten into a thin sheet.

Melting point The temperature at which a solid changes into a liquid. It is the same as the freezing point of the liquid.

Meniscus The curved shape of the surface of a liquid in a narrow tube, caused by capillarity.

Molecule A combination of at least two atoms that forms the smallest unit of a chemical element or compound.

Partial vacuum A region of low atmospheric pressure, especially one in which most of the air has been pumped out.

pascal The standard scientific unit of pressure.

Pressure The amount of force pressing on a particular area.

Solid A state of matter that keeps its own shape (unlike a gas or a liquid).

Surface tension An effect that makes a liquid appear to have a surface "skin."

Thermal conductivity A measure of the ability of a substance to conduct heat.

Thermal A vertical convection current in a gas, usually air.

Turbulence The irregular flow of a fluid moving around an object. It is reduced by streamlining.

Upthrust The apparent loss in weight of a floating object, equal to the buoyant force keeping it afloat.

Vapor Another name for the gas that forms when a liquid boils or evaporates.

Vaporization The change from liquid to gas or vapor on heating.

FURTHER RESEARCH

Books – General

Bloomfield, Louis A. *How Things Work: The Physics of Everyday Life.* Hoboken, NJ: Wiley, 2009.

Bloomfield, Louis A. *How Everything Works: Making Physics Out of the Ordinary.* Hoboken, NJ: Wiley, 2007.

Daintith, John. *A Dictionary of Physics.* New York, NY: Oxford University Press, 2010.

De Pree, Christopher. *Physics Made Simple.* New York, NY: Broadway Books, 2005.

Epstein, Lewis Carroll. *Thinking Physics: Understandable Practical Reality.* San Francisco, CA: Insight Press, 2009.

Glencoe McGraw-Hill. *Introduction to Physical Science.* Blacklick, OH: Glencoe/McGraw-Hill, 2007.

Heilbron, John L. *The Oxford Guide to the History of Physics and Astronomy.* New York, NY: Oxford University Press, 2005.

Holzner, Steve. *Physics Essentials For Dummies.* Hoboken, NJ: For Dummies, 2010.

Jargodzk, Christopher, and Potter, Franklin. *Mad About Physics: Braintwisters, Paradoxes, and Curiosities.* Hoboken, NJ: Wiley, 2000.

Lehrman, Robert L. *E-Z Physics.* Hauppauge, NY: Barron's Educational, 2009.

Lloyd, Sarah. *Physics: IGCSE Revision Guide.* New York, NY: Oxford University Press, 2009.

Suplee, Curt. *Physics in the 20th Century.* New York, NY: Harry N. Abrams, 2002.

Taylor, Charles (ed). *The Kingfisher Science Encyclopedia,* Boston, MA: Kingfisher Books, 2006.

Walker, Jearl. *The Flying Circus of Physics.* Hoboken, NJ: Wiley, 2006.

Watts, Lisa et al. *The Most Explosive Science Book in the Universe... by the Brainwaves.* New York, NY: DK Publishing, 2009.

Zitzewitz, Paul W. *Physics Principles and Problems.* Columbus, OH: McGraw-Hill, 2005.

Books – Matter, Energy and Heat

Basher, Simon, and Green, Dan. *Physics: Why Matter Matters!* Boston, MA: Kingfisher Books, 2008.

Challoner, Jack. *Eyewitness Books: Energy.* New York, NY: DK Publishing, 2000.

Cooper, Christopher. *Eyewitness Books: Matter.* New York, NY: DK Publishing, 2000.

Graybill, George. *Atoms, Molecules & Elements (Matter & Energy).* San Diego, CA: Classroom Complete Press. 2007.

Web Sites

Marvellous machines
www.galaxy.net/~k12/machines/index.shtml
Experiments about simple machines.

How Stuff Works – Physical Science
http://science.howstuffworks.com/physical-science-channel.htm
Topics on all aspects of physics.

PhysLink.com
www.physlink.com/SiteInfo/Index.cfm
Physics and astronomy education, research, and reference.

PhysicsCentral
www.physicscentral.com/about/index.cfm
Education site of the American Physical Society.

Physics 2000
www.colorado.edu/physics/2000/index.pl
An interactive journey through modern physics.

The Why Files
http://whyfiles.org/
The science behind the news.

INDEX